A Creative Approach to Teaching Grammar

The what, why and how of teaching grammar in context

by Peter Burrows

B L O O M S B U R Y

LONDON · OXFORD · NEW YORK · NEW DELHI · SYDNEY

Bloomsbury Education

An imprint of Bloomsbury Publishing Plc

50 Bedford Square
London
WC1B 3DP
UK

1385 Broadway
New York
NY 10018
USA

www.bloomsbury.com

Bloomsbury is a registered trade mark of Bloomsbury Publishing Plc

First published 2014

© Peter Burrows 2014

All rights reserved. No part of this publication may be reproduced in any form or by any means – graphic, electronic, or mechanical, including photocopying, recording, taping or information storage or retrieval systems – without the prior permission in writing from the publishers.

British Library Cataloguing-in-Publication Data

A catalogue record for this book is available from the British Library.

ISBN PB: 978-1-4729-0902-2
ePub: 978-1-4729-0903-9
ePDF: 978-1-4729-0904-6

Library of Congress Cataloging-in-Publication Data

A catalog record for this book is available from the Library of Congress.

5 7 9 10 8 6 4

Typeset by Newgen Knowledge Works (P) Ltd., Chennai, India
Printed and bound by CPI Group (UK) Ltd, Croydon CR0 4YY

This book is produced using paper that is made from wood grown in managed, sustainable forests. It is natural, renewable and recyclable. The logging and manufacturing processes conform to the environmental regulations of the country of origin.

To view more of our titles please visit www.bloomsbury.com

Acknowledgements

I would like to thank all my colleagues within Babcock Four S Education, for their continued support. Thanks also to the Surrey teachers and children with whom I have worked, particularly those at Guildford Grove Primary School.
I am particularly grateful to Elizabeth Corlett: for her inspired leadership; keeping me focussed on teaching and learning; and showing me what is possible in education.
'Where the Wild Things Are' illustration on page 32 reproduced with kind permission of *HarperCollins Publishers*.

Contents

1

Introduction: A pedagogical approach to punctuation and grammar

'The test of successful education is not the amount of knowledge that pupils take away from school, but their appetite to know and their capacity to learn.'

Sir Richard Livingstone, 1941

I attended a Secondary Modern school, where grammar and punctuation were rarely taught. The teacher gave us ideas to write about and off we went. This I found relatively easy but felt at the time, little was being taught. It was only when I reached sixth form that anyone commented on the grammar and punctuation (or lack of it) in my writing. I remember being marched off to see the headteacher with an essay I had written. 'Look, he doesn't even write in sentences,' went up the cry.

Having taught in primary schools for over 20 years, and having been a Literacy Consultant, fortunate enough to observe classroom practice in a number of settings, I wanted to ensure this book was based on research but also offered the busy teacher practical suggestions. This book aims to develop:

- the child's writing as a whole and their punctuation and grammar within this
- the teacher's ability to support children with the *English grammar, punctuation and spelling test* and the 2014 National Curriculum for English through a range of teaching techniques
- classroom dialogue and discussion about grammar
- a clear sequence for teaching grammar and punctuation using the following structure:
  - explicitly teach: within modelled writing
  - practise: through word games and activities
  - apply: when drafting, proofreading and editing.

Using these three techniques it is possible to have a significant impact on both children's grammar and punctuation and their writing as a whole. A balance is found where skills are explicitly taught but within the context of an exciting and interesting curriculum.

How to use this book

This book aims to support the busy teacher with a range of practical activities to help children with grammar and punctuation. Each chapter starts with the key concept and chapter summary. These are then followed by a range of teaching ideas. Initially you might want to dip into the individual activities suggested and that is fine. However, taking time to look at what the research suggests will lead to a much deeper understanding of how best to teach grammar and punctuation.

A new curriculum (2014)

It is first worth considering the present educational climate and how recent recommendations will impact on future teaching. The education system in England is in a process of significant flux and explained below are some of the most relevant and recent changes.

Many people see this new curriculum for 2014 as heralding the return to a more formal, knowledge-based curriculum. Certainly in English, the two appendices, one for spelling and the other for grammar, clearly set out the direction of travel and subject matter to be taught. However, the curriculum for English remains relatively broad and gives teachers considerable freedom to determine the context and content of their English lessons. The creative approaches suggested in this book will fully support the development of the skills needed by the end of the key stage.

> In this chapter you will:
> - **gain a better understanding of the key changes happening in education and their impact on the teaching of grammar**
> - **develop your understanding of the importance of pedagogy in relation to grammar and punctuation**

Greater focus on progress and data

Soon after the introduction of the National Literacy Strategy in 1988, it became apparent that standards in primary children's writing were lower when compared to both reading and mathematics. The situation has changed little over the past few decades. The percentages of pupils achieving the expected level, level 4 or above, in the 2011 Writing Key Stage 2 test was 75%, compared to 84% in reading and 80% in mathematics. Only 69% of boys achieved national expectations in writing.

A number of initiatives, including the Primary Framework have tried to improve standards but without significant impact. The first Ofsted report *National Literacy Strategy: an interim evaluation* (1999) commented that the results of the writing tests were worrying. Ofsted commissioned a further report, *The Teaching of Writing in Primary Schools: Could do better* (2000). There were two main findings: there was still insufficient teaching of writing; and where writing was taught, there were significant weaknesses in too many lessons. More recent reports show little has changed and that standards of literacy are not keeping up with our international competitors.

In the *Organisation for Economic Cooperation and Development survey for the Programme for International Student Assessment* (2006), Britain fell from seventh to seventeenth place in literacy. This survey confirms that some persistent issues remain, including:

- the gap between girls and boys achievement, especially in writing
- evidence of lower standards overall in writing
- poorer performance in English by pupils from disadvantaged backgrounds or those eligible for free school meals.

Changes in the school inspection system

Recently the term 'satisfactory' has been changed to 'requires improvement'; the number of times schools can be deemed to 'require improvement' has been limited to two consecutive inspections, before they are judged 'inadequate' and deemed to require 'special measures'. More emphasis is placed on the quality of teaching and an important form of evidence is the children's books and progress they have made.

Common findings from recent Ofsted inspections include:

- the need to improve basic skills including spelling, grammar and punctuation
- work needs to be better matched to the needs of the pupils
- teachers' marking does not always provide pupils with enough guidance on how to improve their work
- expectations, and the level of engagement and challenge, is not high enough
- pupils do not have enough opportunities to develop their writing skills.

Pupil premium

The pupil premium is an additional funding given to schools so that they can support their disadvantaged pupils and close the attainment gap with their peers. Schools are free to decide how to use the pupil premium but are held accountable for the decisions they make. This group of pupils often struggle with writing, especially in relation to language and sentence structure.

Assessment

In 2012, significant changes to the Key Stage 2 assessment arrangements were introduced. Schools were no longer required to administer a writing test for external marking. Under the new system, teachers are expected to look at a range of evidence to give the child an overall level. This has largely been welcomed by teachers and resulted in less prescriptive teaching.

Changes in testing arrangements

In 2011 we saw the introduction of the Phonics Screening Check and in 2013 the *English grammar, punctuation and spelling test* was introduced. Results are published separately to reading and writing but it is likely that these tests will become more significant in future years. In the *English grammar, punctuation and spelling test* only 74% achieved level 4 or above, which means that one in four children did not achieve the expected level. The figure for boys is even worse: only 69% achieved level 4 or above. Performance is published by Ofsted RAISE online (Reporting and Analysis for Improvement through School Self-Evaluation).

Also National Curriculum levels will be discontinued, when new Programmes of Study (PoS) become statutory. These are structured to require assessment of 'readiness to progress' at the end of key stages, rather than giving overall levels. However, ongoing assessment will still be seen as a crucial part of effective teaching and it will be up to schools to decide what form this takes. Appendix 1 (page 79) offers a possible way of doing this in relation to punctuation and grammar, as explained in Chapter 4 (page 21).

An increased emphasis on pedagogy and research

At a time of so much change it is important that schools consider their overall aims and priorities. Schools will need to ensure that children receive an exciting curriculum that supports, engages and challenges, while maintaining good practice that they know works. New curriculums come and go, but good schools thrive despite the changes. They stick to their principles, putting pedagogy, and teaching and learning first.

'Broadly speaking, pedagogy is the why, what and how of teaching,' (Cambridge Review 2009). It is to do with teaching and learning but more, it is teaching and learning based on research, culture and the ethos of the school. Pedagogy is the craft of teaching which permeates all aspects of the curriculum and is the antidote to decontextualised, compartmentalised activities. There are a number of key pedagogies that deserve attention, including the development of dialogic talk, modelled and guided work and questioning and feedback. These cut across the content of teaching. Focussing on such aspects will impact on grammar but also across the whole curriculum.

The teaching of grammar and punctuation needs to be based upon sound subject knowledge and repertoire, where a number of techniques are known and used, rather than on recipes handed down from above. Grammar is used all the time, in talk and within all subjects. A pedagogy of grammar is one that doesn't see grammar as a decontextualised, worksheet-style activity, where children are required to identify and fill in adjectives and adverbs. It is a dynamic subject that embeds everything that is done in school.

Pupils should be taught to control their speaking and writing consciously and to use standard English. This is the approach that the new curriculum endorses: 'They should be taught to use the elements of spelling, grammar, punctuation and 'language about language' listed. This is not intended to constrain or restrict teachers' creativity, but simply to provide the structure on which they can construct exciting lessons.' (*The National Curriculum in England Key Stages 1 and 2 framework document* p15: Department of Education 2013).

In the following chapters, I will explore the pedagogy of punctuation and grammar. First I will consider what research has to tell us, before moving on to consider grammar and talk. Then I explore the recommended teaching sequence including: modelled writing; sentence games and activities; and editing and proofreading. Finally grammar is considered in relation to two schools: one where many pupils are from disadvantaged backgrounds and eligible for pupil premium and the other focuses on a school with more able children.

2
Research and grammar

To parse or not to pass?

Write the correction making sure the verb matches the tense.
I am putting on my shoes and I will <u>have been</u> for a walk in the park right now!   1 mark

---

Key concept

The traditional activity of parsing, where pupils are given a sentence and asked to identify parts of speech, analyse clauses and fill in missing words, is back in the form of the *English grammar, punctuation and spelling test*. The example above is taken from the Government's 2012 example paper, which implements the recommendation of Lord Bew's review, that writing composition should be subject to teacher assessment only, with the more 'technical' aspects of English being assessed via an externally marked test.

One of the main concerns within schools is what the test means in relation to classroom practice. What is the best way to teach grammar so that children write well but also make good progress within the PoS and the *English grammar, punctuation and spelling test*? In this chapter I will explore some of the definitions and research into grammar.

In this chapter you will:

- **develop a clear definition of what grammar is and how it has developed over the centuries**
- **know how recent research suggests how best to teach grammar and punctuation**

Start from your own beliefs

'For a tree to become tall it must grow tough roots amongst the rocks.'

Friedrich Nietzsche

It is first useful to explore our own thoughts and feelings on the subject of grammar and punctuation. I remember being involved with setting up a new school in an area of high social deprivation. Everyone wanted to get in and tell the school how it should be done. The headteacher however stuck to her own principles. We had to develop our own ethos first; the way we did things on a day-to-day basis. All new initiatives were filtered and adapted to the clear aims of the school, which I still remember to this day. Key priorities included: developing high aspirations; respect for all; life-long learning and empowerment. Too often I hear people trying to tell a school how they should do things and rarely does it work. Hold true to what you know is right.

Consider the following statements and prioritise them in relation to grammar and punctuation:

Teacher's subject knowledge is crucial when teaching grammar.	It is important to teach grammar in context, within children's everyday writing.	Grammar should be taught through modelled and guided writing.
Children need a range of activities where they play with language e.g. adding verbs, adjectives, etc.	Children need to proofread and edit their own writing.	Assessment for learning and progression in grammar need careful consideration.
Little and often works well.	Grammar needs to be taught rather than caught.	Teacher's need to concentrate on the grammar used in children's talk.

There are no right or wrong answers to this exercise and the majority of statements are hard to argue against in isolation. However, debate about grammar often becomes polarised, between those wanting a return to 'traditional' teaching methods and formal grammar, while others passionately focus on creativity and composition. However, is there a middle more creative approach, where grammar is taught within whole texts but supported through short sessions, where children play with sentence structure? The teaching sequence suggested in this book hopefully goes some way towards this. But first let us consider what grammar is and what the research tells us.

What is grammar?

In classical Greek, grammar was concerned with three elements:

Syntax – the rules by which words are combined into larger structures such as phrases, clauses and sentences, and how these relationships are indicated.

Morphology – the rules and principles of the structure and changes in word formation.

Semantics – the relationship between words, sentences and their meanings.

This definition held true in Medieval Europe where the principles and structures of Latin were applied to English, despite the differences between the two languages. Bear in mind that English did not exist as a separate subject until the mid-nineteenth century. It was in the early part of the twentieth century, when the teaching of grammar really took off. One of the main concerns was the application of a set of rules to ensure correct sentence construction. This 'traditional formal grammar' was associated with books, containing drills on parsing: the identifying of parts of speech and clause analysis. It persisted until the early 1960's, when research findings, which are perhaps now less convincing, claimed that grammar teaching failed to improve children's writing.

Grammar in education

More recent definitions of grammar come from the linguists rather than education. Michael Halliday introduced the term 'systemic-functional grammar', which looks at grammar in terms of meaning – systemic refers to grammar being spread throughout the whole text. This would seem to offer a more useful definition for teachers to work with, a more top down approach where it is the function, or job of the word within the sentence or text, that is most important. For example, in the sentence 'The butcher began to <u>slice</u> the ham,' the function of the word 'slice' is to signify what the butcher is doing – it is a verb. However in the sentence 'Tom looked at the cake and then helped himself to a large <u>slice</u>,' the job of the word 'slice' is as the object of the sentence – it is a noun.

Functional grammar goes further than just looking at a word within a sentence. Through the development of genre theory, teachers are able to look at the features of whole texts and then explore the best words and phrases to use. All communication has a function e.g. to explain, disagree or persuade. The speaker or writer chooses the grammar according to the situation. This has become popular in the teaching of literacy, where for example children look at the features of different styles of writing and incorporate them into their own work.

The *English grammar, punctuation and spelling test* itself includes questions that assess sentence, grammar, punctuation and vocabulary, so these are areas on which I will focus in this book. For the purpose of this book, grammar is defined as a set of rules, dependent upon the form of speaking and writing intended, which structure the sequence within and between words. Grammar is like looking under the bonnet of language, to see how it works. When grammar is mentioned, the study of punctuation is included. 'Sentences actively create sense in language and the business of the study of sentences, is the study of grammar,' (*Grammar for Writing*, p7 Department for Education and Employment (2000)).

How to teach grammar: the great debate

Opinion on how best to teach grammar is greatly divided. On the one hand, there are those that advocate traditional formal activities and the direct teaching of grammar. However, others argue that the teaching of grammar can have a detrimental and demotivating affect. Two pieces of influential research help illustrate this conflict.

Harris, in the 1960's, compared two groups of children: one were taught grammar using exercises from a standard textbook and the other were not. He found that the grammar group scored more highly in a grammar test but this was not reflected in their writing. He concluded, that control and accuracy of written language were more likely to be achieved by having more practice in writing, rather than being taught traditional formal grammar. Furthermore he stated, 'It seems safe to infer that the study of English grammar has a negligible or even harmful effect upon the correctness of children's writing,' (Harris, 1965, in *The Grammar Papers*, 1998 p47). As a result, the teaching of formal grammar was stopped in the majority of schools, so that we now have a generation of teachers who do not know grammatical rules and whose subject knowledge is weak.

However in the 1990's, Tomlinson turned these findings on their head in *The Grammar Papers*. He pointed out that the non-grammar group were being taught grammar: the teachers taught sentence and paragraph structure and how to link ideas and errors were corrected by example, rather than referring to grammatical categories. He therefore concluded that looking at isolated words, and being able to say what part of speech they are, is not a good way to teach grammatical knowledge. Earlier research, he concluded, was not an argument for not teaching grammar, looking at the whole text and sentence structure would have a more positive impact.

This approach was further developed through the work of Wray and Lewis (1995) on genre theory, which identified the larger structure features within whole texts. For example, recounts are written in the past tense using time connectives, with a particular person as the subject; instructions are more likely to be written in the present tense, in the second person and start with an imperative verb. This approach was adopted within *Grammar for Writing* (DfEE, 2000), which was a popular document with teachers. While there was an element of a return to formal grammar, the focus was more on the improvement of sentence structure and increased language awareness to help pupils to improve their writing. It struck a middle path, where both spoken and written language was discussed using traditional terminology. It was hoped that explicitly teaching grammatical terms would help children to discuss language and make informed choices when writing. Certainly, approaches such as intervening at the point of writing, where children rehearse sentences orally, or with the teacher prior to writing, seem to impact in the classroom.

The current view

More recent research, undertaken by Andrews R, et al (2004), confirms these earlier findings. This was the most extensive review to date of the effect of grammar teaching on the accuracy and quality of written composition; the initial search identified 4,691 papers to analyse. On the basis of the results there were two key findings:

- Teaching of formal grammar by itself was ineffective; pupils taught using formal grammar found lessons more repetitive and there was little impact on children's writing.
- The second finding is more encouraging – 'the teaching of sentence combining, is one of probably a number of methods, that is effective.' (p39).

Sentence combining is defined as a range of practical techniques for moving from existing simple sentences to compound and complex ones. F. O'Hare's (1973) study, for example, showed that with an experimental group using sentence combining, performance exceeded that of the control group. They performed at a syntactic maturity level four years above expected. The technique is explored further within the sentence games in Chapter 6 of this book. What distinguishes sentence combining from traditional formal grammar is that it is practical, and is not concerned with the teaching of a set of rules. Such activities are practical and fun, yet through the discussion on how sentences are combined, both the knowledge and skills needed for the *English grammar, punctuation and spelling test* and 2014 National Curriculum for English are developed.

Research shows that the two aspects of grammar often debated do not have to be mutually exclusive. The argument needs to focus not on should grammar be taught, but on what form of grammar teaching will have most impact? Exploring grammatical structures in context, and playing with language through sentence games while using the correct grammatical terminology, will impact on children's writing. So while grammar can be tested through the activities suggested in the *English grammar, punctuation and spelling test* it is not the best way to teach it. 'Discrete teaching of parts of speech and parsing in de-contextualised exercise form is not a particularly effective activity. . . There is no evidence that knowledge acquired in this way transfers to writing competence,' (*The Grammar Papers* 1998, p55). This is not to say that the testing of grammar is not useful, just that it is not the best the way to teach it.

The Department for Education's most recent report into recent research and the teaching of writing further supports these findings. 'The contextualised teaching of grammar has also a significantly positive effect on pupils' writing development. The approach is more effective for the most able writers.' (p3 Myhill et al, within *What is the Research Evidence on Writing?* 2012). The recommendation in this book is that grammar and punctuation is explicitly taught and modelled within an exciting and motivating curriculum. With the importance placed on the grammar and punctuation test, the stakes are too high not to. Specific skills must be taught, but this needs to be done in context, in a way that stimulates and motivates all pupils.

3
The importance of talk and grammar

'The biggest enemy to learning is the talking teacher.'

John Holt 1964

Key concept

The importance of talk cannot be underestimated when it comes to teaching grammar.

In this chapter you will:

- **understand how the differences in language development experienced in the classroom impact on pupil's grammar**
- **realise how language and real experiences help develop children's thinking**
- **be able to use a range of practical talk and drama activities through which grammar can be explored in context**

Talk and the 2014 curriculum

The 2014 National Curriculum for English clearly states that grammar should be taught in context and specifically within speaking and listening. 'The grammar of our first language is learned naturally and implicitly through interactions with other speakers and from reading. Explicit knowledge of grammar is, however, very important, as it gives us more conscious control and choice in our language. Building this knowledge is best achieved through a focus on grammar within the teaching of reading, writing and speaking.' (Department for Education, *The National Curriculum in England Key stages 1 and 2 framework document* (2013) p74)

If children cannot talk in sentences, or use grammatically accurate clauses, they will be unable to do so in their writing. Questions relating to grammar are also common in the *English grammar, punctuation and spelling test*, such as 'I hasn't got any money' (2013). If such statements are not picked up in the child's talk, it is unlikely that they will be able to correct it in their writing.

The differences in language among a group of children within a classroom can be huge. By the age of 4, a child from a home receiving welfare benefits will have heard 6.5 million words, compared to 45 million words for a child from a professional family (Hart B and Risley T 1995). This is a huge difference in quantity, but the quality of the talk heard is also hugely influential. In addition to this it is through language we develop our ideas and thoughts.

Edgar Dale's 'Cone of Experience' (1969)

This diagram above helps illustrate the point (some versions put percentages alongside the various elements but this was always meant to be a visual metaphor, rather than an exact representation). The point is that we learn far more from what we discuss and do, rather than just hear and see. As a teacher it does feel instinctively right: active participation through discussion, has a significant impact on how children learn. Children need to be engaged in their own learning and not be passive recipients. Being from the north of England myself, regional dialects are acceptable but poor grammar is not; children need to be taught that phrases such as 'she done it,' or 'they was going,' will influence how they are perceived.

Tandy and Howell (2008), stress the importance of experience, particularly when writing non-fiction. They use the analogy of an iceberg, with the skills we assess, including spelling, punctuation and text structure on top. However, we also need to attend to what sits below the iceberg, which include experiences, discussion, reading and observation. We can all think of examples of writing where the emphasis on the functional features of grammar has become too top heavy, at the expense of meaning. The child may be trying hard, using complex sentences, a range of connectives, similes and semi-colons – yet the writing doesn't say anything or make sense.

For writing children need real experiences and to have a clear audience and purpose in mind. A child can be shown a picture of a leaf but if they go out to touch and smell it, feel it crinkle in their hands and throw handfuls into the air, the quality of writing will be far more descriptive. The scope of this book is not one where we can go into the full range of drama and talk activities but a few are recommended here that will impact particularly on grammar. It is important to be objective-led when planning.

The table opposite shows key PoS (2014) in relation to grammar and talk to which games and activities can be matched.

Year 1	Year 2	Year 3/4	Year 5/6
Say out loud what they are going to write about. Compose a sentence orally before writing it. Sequence sentences to form short narratives. Re-read what they have written to check that it makes sense.	Write down ideas and/ or key words, including new vocabulary. Re-read to check that their writing makes sense and that verbs to indicate time are used correctly and consistently, including verbs in the continuous form.	Discuss writing similar to that which they are planning to write in order to understand and learn from its structure, vocabulary and grammar. Discuss and record ideas. Compose and rehearse sentences orally (including dialogue), progressively building a varied and rich vocabulary and an increasing range of sentence structures.	Identify the audience and purpose of the writing, selecting the appropriate form and using other similar writing as models for their own. Note and develop initial ideas, drawing on reading and research where necessary. Consider how authors have developed characters and settings in what they have read, listened to or seen performed. Perform their own compositions, using appropriate intonation, volume, and movement.

Teaching ideas

Think, pair, share

Think, pair share is a technique that stops the minority dominating the class while the rest turn off and it also helps to structure the talk. It develops collaborative and independent learning and is easy to use on the spur of the moment.

The teacher poses a problem or asks an open-ended question, to which there may be a variety of answers. Pupils are given 'think time' and then turn to face their learning partner to share, discuss and clarify their thinking. They then share ideas with another pair, or with the whole class. The element that is often missing is the think time but this is an essential part of the process. Children need the opportunity to consider and reflect on the question themselves, before discussion begins. Research tells us we need time to mentally 'chew over' new ideas in order to store them in memory.

I remember one girl in particular, Nadine, her written work was of a good standard but as with many children who have English as an additional language, verb tenses were often confused. She fell into the category of an 'invisible child': the sort of child who sits quietly in the room and is never a problem. However her language was not being developed. The combination of a talk programme and think, pair, share, gave her the opportunity to elaborate on her ideas and develop the technical language she needed. Many of the activities below were used.

Talk frames

The new PoS include the need for children to discuss writing, in order to understand and learn from its structure, vocabulary and grammar. One technique to develop this is the use of visual planning devices, which have become known as skeleton frames. While as teachers, we need to be careful not to overly emphasise genre at the expense of experience, they still offer a useful scaffold, especially in relation to talk. The different text types have their own characteristic language features. 'Many children (especially boys) find it helpful to make this kind of 'big picture' record, so they have an overview of the whole piece of writing. . .' (Sue Palmer 2003).

The examples below show possible starting points.

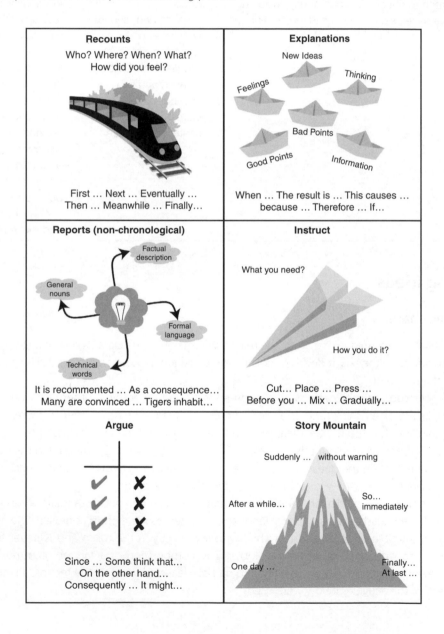

When children are planning their writing they can use the appropriate talk frame as shown opposite. So if writing recounts, the child would first talk through their ideas with a partner. The other child can check that they have enough information and haven't missed anything out. For example they might ask: Who did you go with? The features and grammar of each text type is further explained below.

Recounts: The image used is that of a journey. Recounts are chronological and written in the past tense using connectives that signal time. They focus on individual or group participants, for example I, we, or they. Encourage the use of questions, pronouns, consistency in tense and a range of connectives.

Reports (non-chronological): With non-fiction, children need to research, make notes and then practise the language structures orally. Reports are generally written in the present tense and use the passive voice, where the object of a sentence is placed first, for example: *The book was read by the boy*, rather than: *The boy read the book*. They focus on generic subjects e.g. 'the children', rather than 'Sam'. Encourage the use of descriptive language, including the language of comparison and contrast for precision, rather than to create an effect or emotion.

Argue: Children can debate issues in the classroom using the present tense. Encourage the use of unspecified numbers and generic subjects, for example 'many people'. A range of causal connectives should be included.

Many texts use a combination of genres, for example, in one of my favourite cookbooks Jamie Oliver writes, 'A bowl of this spectacular soup feels like a cuddle from your granny.' This doesn't follow the rules for instructions and has more in common with persuasive texts, however it does add to the richness of the writing. We don't want to produce a strait-jacket for our children, with a set of mechanical rules that stifles independence. However talk frames do help children rehearse language structures and are useful in their own right, or as a pre-writing activity.

Explanations: De Bono's thinking hats can be useful in helping children organise and develop their ideas. Explanations are generally written in the present tense and use both time and causal connectives. Encourage the use of language that describes compares and analyses. Comparatives such as smaller and smallest can be introduced, along with superlatives such as 'best'.

Instruct: Children can first carry out the activity and explain it to a friend using imperative verbs, e.g. *Fold the paper*. Encourage the use of adverbs and adjectives for precision, e.g. *Carefully measure ten grams*.

Story telling

It is important that children develop their understanding of stories and the language used, so that it is reflected in their writing. A simple way to get children to retell a story is to give them four or five pictures to sequence, then as a group they use these to retell the story.

Another technique is story mapping. Pie Corbett is a big advocate of this technique, where through learning stories off by heart, children learn the language structures used and then apply this grammatical knowledge within their writing. Children listen to the story and then learn to retell it using a story map and so internalise its structure. Traditional tales such as 'Little Red Riding Hood' are ideal as a starting point but any good quality short story can be used. Picture books work particularly well, such as *Mrs Armitage on Wheels* by Quentin Blake (Red Fox). The teacher or the children first produce a map representing the story and then add key words and phrases to help with the retelling.

The example below is for a retelling of the Greek myth Arachne. Children use the phrases beneath to help them retell the story. Once they have started to internalise the story structure they are ready to imitate. The basic story line remains the same but an element is changed, so for example the story is set in modern times or the myth tells the story of the first dolphin.

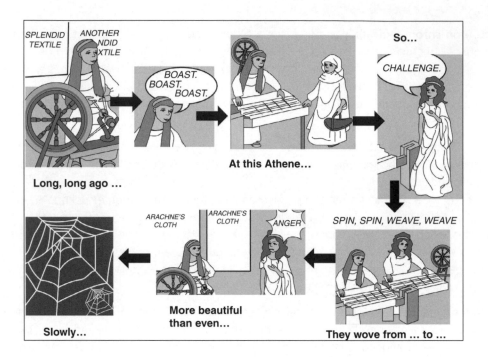

Each part of the story will have its own language structure. The opening often describes the setting and introduces the main character and therefore needs to use adjectives and expanded noun phrases. Then the build-up takes the main character from where the story starts to where the main dilemma will take place: dialogue can be used effectively to develop characterisation and relationships. In the main dilemma, suspense can be built through using short sentences for impact and hiding what is about to happen next. The ending is often reflective, referring back to the start of the story or explaining how the character has changed.

Book talk

Children need to be given plenty of time to reflect on their reading and one good strategy to enable this is book talk. This is a strategy used by Aidan Chambers and further developed by Pie Corbett. I am also pleased to see that its importance is recognised within the 2014 National Curriculum for English. Children are encouraged to 'participate in discussion about books, poems and other works that are read to them and those that they can read for themselves, taking turns and listening to what others say.' (Department for Education, *The National Curriculum in England Key stages 1 and 2 framework document* (2013) p28)

The first stage is to elicit a response. So, after reading, rather than launching into specific questioning, we first want to elicit the children's initial thoughts and ideas, through questions such as: Tell me what you thought, or what did you picture? Children can be asked to describe, reflect and speculate on what happened.

The next stage is to get children to expand on their response through discussion such as: Tell me more about . . . Children can be asked to clarify their thinking and any puzzles can be discussed.

Finally children are asked to discuss any other possible views and ideas about the text. Connections can be made, linking elements of the text together or thinking about other texts or their own experiences. Another good strategy related to books is 'magpieing'. Here children are asked to collect words and phrases that they might want to use within their own writing.

Books should first be enjoyed for their own sake and some discussion about grammatical features will arise naturally relating to audience and purpose. Questioning specific to grammar can also be further developed. Bloom's Taxonomy was used in the creation of the questions used for the *English grammar, punctuation and spelling test*. I have related the example below to grammar.

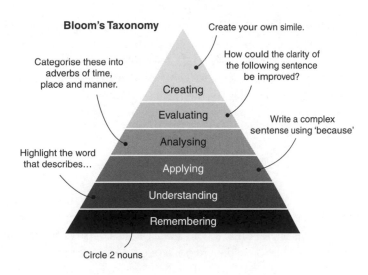

A number of further drama techniques can be used that help focus on the use of grammar within talk.

Hot seating

This technique is often used in schools: the teacher becomes the character in the 'hot seat' and the children ask questions. It can be used effectively for both non-fiction and fiction. I remember the children used to love, for example, when I took on the role of the Victorian engineer Brunel, complete with large top hat and strong northern accent.

Hot seating can be used even more powerfully when working with groups of children so that they are allowed to take more control. The children brainstorm possible questions to ask and then one of them takes on the role of the character while the others ask questions. Children sometimes find it difficult to ask questions initially, so having question cards on the table can be useful. These might include: Where? When? Why? How? What? or Should? So for example, the child might come up with '**How**. . . did the room change?' in response to reading *Where the Wild Things Are* by Maurice Sendak (1963). Or when reading *Harry Potter and the Philosopher's Stone* by J.K. Rowling (1997) they might ask the question '**What**. . . do you think about Dudley?' One of the children would them take on the role of Harry and answer. When hot seating there are a number of language features to explore including the use of questioning and answering in sentences and justifying viewpoint through the use of causal connectives such as 'because' and 'therefore'.

Freeze frames and thought tracking

Children take on roles to create a still image from a story and then explore what each character might be thinking or saying. Picture books are ideal as children can recreate and then act out the scene. So after reading *Where the Wild Things Are* (1963) the children might decide to create the scene where Max tames the Wild Things. One child takes the role of Max and two others become the Wild Things. They then explore what each character might be thinking or saying and this then can be used to create a short improvisation.

Once children get used to this technique it can be used again and again. I remember when guided reading with Year 5, groups would ask me if they could recreate various scenes. This was drama in context in the classroom, not a special one off event for which the hall needed to be booked. I remember them reading *Harry Potter and the Philosopher's Stone* (1997) for example and then creating the train scene where Harry meets Ron and Malfoy (p81, 82). The grammar used within their presentation was specifically discussed in context. The children discussed how Malfoy would say certain phrases and then considered the punctuation to use to make this clear.

Conscience alley

Here a moment in a story or a real life dilemma is chosen. Children then take opposing sides and create statements that support their point of view. It is rather like the old cartoons, where the character has a devil on one shoulder and angel on the other arguing for a certain course of action. Again consider using this for both fiction and non-fiction. So children might argue for and against the building of yet another supermarket in the area. Within a story such as *Jack and the Beanstalk* the dilemma: Should Jack swap his cow for some magic beans? might be used. Children are then put into two teams to come up with their suggestions. Statements the children could come up with might include 'Your mum will be so cross,' or 'Take a chance; you never know what might happen.' The children then form two lines facing each other. One child takes the role of Jack and walks through while the others whisper their statements for and against the decision. Another example I have seen being used to great effect was using the book *Leon and the Place Between* by Graham Baker-Smith (2008). Children argued as to whether Leon should step into the Magic Box or not. There was a lot of discussion about the language being used, including the use of persuasive language and causal connectives to extend their reasoning.

Role on the wall

A body shape is drawn onto a piece of paper and the children then describe the character's appearance and write key facts around the outside. Within the shape they concentrate more on the character's personality. What do they like/dislike? Are they bossy, a born leader or adventurous? Would you like them as a friend? In cross curricular work for example, the children might be finding out about a Roman soldier defending Hadrian's Wall. They can discuss how the character feels, why he joined the army and how others might feel about him. In terms of grammar, this is an ideal opportunity to focus on descriptive language including adjectives and expanded noun phrases. Complex sentences can be used to give further information about the character.

With all the activities suggested, the real skill is intervening so as to develop the language and vocabulary being used. Recent Ofsted reports emphasise the importance of talk. 'Good-quality oral work engages pupils, including boys and pupils who might otherwise take little interest, and yields benefits in all areas of English,' (*Excellence in English*, 2011 p7). The importance of talk in developing children's grammar cannot be underestimated.

4
The teaching sequence and progression in grammar

A presentational approach, where the teacher acts as a font of all knowledge, explaining parts of speech and giving exercises to mark and hand back, will have little impact on children's writing.

Key concept

Children need to work through the whole process of writing: planning; drafting; revising; proofreading and editing their work. They need to act like real writers to develop the craft of writing. This is the writing workshop approach advocated in this book, where both teacher and child act as writing professionals, discussing the process of writing and developing language within the process. Grammar is explicitly taught within the process and practised through short games and activities. The grammar and punctuation needed to achieve well within the *English grammar, punctuation and spelling test* and the 2014 National Curriculum for English is made explicit within this process.

In this chapter you will:

- **learn how to engage pupil's interest in writing and grammar through a writing workshop approach**
- **understand the benefits of using the recommended teaching sequence: teach, practise and apply**
- **be able to use the progression in grammar grids to support learning and differentiation**

Writing workshop

Excellence in English (Ofsted, 2011) looked at how writing workshops were used within one outstanding primary school. 'It is a step-by-step approach with pupils and teachers working together on constructing a piece of writing. In each lesson, the pupils work through a series of exercises before moving to a longer piece which is sharply focused on specific criteria. The pupils' work, with its crossings-out and additions, shows how well these pupils operate as real writers, constantly looking to rewrite and improve', (p10).

This creative approach developed teachers' own confidence as writers and is the antithesis to dull, out of context activities. However it is not the norm, as reported in Ofsted's *Moving English Forward* (2012), which found in many schools that there was:

- 'too little choice for pupils in the topics for writing
- too few real audiences and purposes for writing
- too few opportunities for pupils to complete extended writing
- too little time in lessons to complete writing tasks
- too little emphasis on creative and imaginative tasks
- too little emphasis on the teaching of editing and redrafting.'

The recommended process of writing starts with the child at the centre, taking into account their experiences and feelings. The children collaborate, reflect and discuss their learning. Discussion with the teacher and between pupils is encouraged and the difference between spoken and written language acknowledged.

Knowledge versus skills

The writing workshop approach to grammar does not mean that knowledge is not explicitly taught. Just that it is done so within the context of pupil's everyday talk, reading and writing.

The swing from one extreme to another is often not helpful in education but the debate between knowledge and skills is of particular relevance to the teaching of grammar. Advocates such as E.D. Hirsch in the United States, argue for a more knowledge based curriculum. Certainly we need to sit up and notice when something appears to work. Massachusetts, where the Hirsch Core Knowledge Curriculum has been widely adopted, regularly outperforms other U.S. States. What might be the advantage of knowledge based curriculum? Might boys, who often prefer the accumulation of knowledge and facts benefit?

Certainly the New English Curriculum appears to be more knowledge based, particularly in relation to grammar and punctuation. Pupil's knowledge of key aspects can, and will, be tested. While knowing doesn't always relate to using, it is a first step in the right direction. Many times, when observing in a classroom, I see the child has a target, such as to use complex sentences. However when discussing this, it soon becomes apparent that the child cannot identify, never mind use one. Knowledge does need to be taught and explained but then also needs to be practised if such knowledge is to be retained. This is the approach adopted in this book. Knowledge is explicitly taught and then practised and applied in context.

Teach, practise and apply

In relation to grammar the sequence recommended is one of teach, practise and apply.

Teach

Through modelled writing grammar is explicitly taught in context using quality texts, children's own experiences and cross-curricular work. Using Assessment for Learning (AfL), key aspects of grammar are identified and then taught. These aspects become embedded within the success criteria of the lesson and then applied in independent work.

Practise

Children then practise the skills taught, through short games and activities. Little and often works well here. When it comes to secretarial skills, including punctuation and sentence structure, children need to embed the skills taught. Pie Corbett uses the image of a wheat field to illustrate the point: if you walk through the field on one day, you will not leave any imprint, it is only by walking the same route every day that a path is made. The process is the same with the basics of grammar. Children need to practise the skills on a regular basis. It is recommended that this is done as a quick five to ten minute warm-up sessions, taking a sentence and playing around with it. Activities such as changing the verb or adding phrases helps to reinforce skills taught in the modelled sessions.

Apply

Finally children develop their work and apply the skills taught through proofreading and editing. Plenty of time is given for drafting their work, while the teacher works with a group on guided writing. The marking and feedback the teacher gives in relation to grammar is crucial to the whole process and children are expected to respond to comments and make improvements.

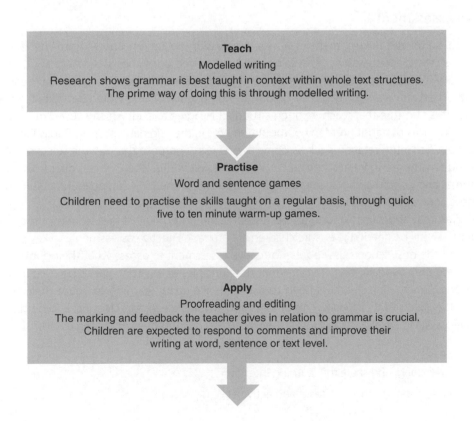

Teach
Modelled writing
Research shows grammar is best taught in context within whole text structures.
The prime way of doing this is through modelled writing.

Practise
Word and sentence games
Children need to practise the skills taught on a regular basis, through quick
five to ten minute warm-up games.

Apply
Proofreading and editing
The marking and feedback the teacher gives in relation to grammar is crucial.
Children are expected to respond to comments and improve their
writing at word, sentence or text level.

Progression in punctuation and grammar

Appendix 1 (page 79) shows the progression in grammar and punctuation, which is based and developed from:

- Appendix 2 from the 2014 National Curriculum for English
- the updated writing level descriptors from the Standards and Testing Agency (STA) 2013
- *English Grammar, Punctuation and Spelling Test Performance Descriptors* (STA) 2013.

The table is divided into six monthly punctuation and grammar ages, so that progress can be tracked within the school. This document should be used for ongoing formative assessment and to inform planning and children's next steps.

But why should we replace the existing levelling system with a progression document? Firstly, this is in line with Lord Bew's Review (2011), which recommended that writing composition should be subject to teacher assessment only, with the more 'technical' aspects of English assessed separately. This is because grammar is much more concrete and easy to test, so leaving the assessment of composition to teacher assessment. This is not to downplay the importance of composition and effect, just that its assessment is more subjective. Grammar still needs to be taught in context, with children being encouraged to choose topics that interest them, using real experiences or quality texts.

Effective assessment

Another reason for the development of a new progression document comes from the fact that it is intended that the present system of levelling will be removed once the 2014 National Curriculum for English is fully introduced. It is claimed that the present system has become overly burdensome and complicated. Certainly a system based on grammar and punctuation age would be easier to understand for parents. It is also true that teachers often struggled to agree a level, which caused many problems, particularly in terms of transition. Many of the statements in the original Assessing Pupils' Progress (APP) grids were open to interpretation, such as, 'some awareness of purpose through the selection of relevant content and an attempt to interest the reader.' While this was within level 3, it could be true of any level. The grammar and punctuation statements from Appendix 2 of the 2014 National Curriculum for English are far more concrete.

While grammar and punctuation can be tested at the end of key stages, some form of formative assessment will still be needed to ensure children are on track. Effective assessment is a key part of good teaching and the best schools use regular formative assessment to assess what their pupils know and identify where they need support. It is vital that the principles of AfL continue to be used in relation to grammar and punctuation. Teachers need to use evidence about learning to adapt their teaching so as to meet the needs of their pupils. This process also ensures meaningful feedback to both pupils and parents. Dylan Wiliam, joint author of *Inside the Black Box*, highlights five key strategies to ensure effective learning:

- 'Clarify, understand, and share the learning intention.
- Generate classroom discussions, tasks and activities.

- Provide feedback that moves learners forward.
- Develop students as learning resources for one another through collaborative learning, reciprocal teaching, and peer-assessment.
- Develop students as owners of their own learning, developing metacognition, motivation and self-assessment.'

The intention of removing the present levelling system is to give schools greater autonomy over curriculum and assessment, so that teaching focuses more on the content rather than on a set of level descriptors. Schools will need to still track progress but are free to decide how best to do this. 'Schools will be free to design their approaches to assessment, to support pupil attainment and progression. The assessment framework must be built into the school curriculum, so that schools can check what pupils have learned and whether they are on track to meet expectations at the end of the key stage, and so that they can report regularly to parents,' (*Primary Assessment and Accountability Under the New National Curriculum* 2013 p8). As the progression in grammar grid (Appendix 1 page 79) is based on the detail given in Appendix 2 of the 2014 National Curriculum for English it is much better matched to it.

Levels have been indicated

It is still possible to match the progression grids to level descriptors if a school wishes. This follows the recommendations made in Report of the NAHT Commission on Assessment (February 2014).

> "There will be a mixed economy in most schools as they see current pupils through the final years of the old system and engage with the new curriculum. Schools are advised to evolve new structures, rather than try to cope with a barren landscape devoid of the old." (p4)

The main message is that schools do not need to panic. The current forms of assessment, using levels, will still be relevant for tracking progress and for accountability at the end of KS1 and KS2 until July 2015. While testing might become more prominent in the future, on-going formative assessment, that is used to evaluate progress and diagnose the needs of pupils, is still an important aspect of good teaching. In the interim, levels are therefore indicated. However it should be realised that pitch and expectation is higher due to the demands of the new curriculum. As teachers become more familiar with the document and terminology involved, the use of levels can be removed and the Punctuation and Grammar age referred to instead.

I have also indicated APS which are now widely used in school and by Ofsted to track progress. So within level 3 for example:

- 3c would be working just within the level (APS19)
- 3b would be working securely within the level (APS 21)
- 3a would be working at the top of the level (APS 23).

However, it should be realised that pitch and expectation is higher due to the demands of the new curriculum.

Know, apply and understand

The key purpose of the progression in grammar grids is so that pupils know, apply and understand the skills and processes specified in the PoS. With the introduction of the 2014 National Curriculum for English it is important that schools first discuss the basic principles and aims involved and ask what they are trying to achieve through it. It must be remembered, no curriculum is complete in itself. It provides just one element in the education of every child and time can be taken to '. . .range beyond its specifications.' *(What is the research evidence on writing?* Education Standards Research Team, DfE 2012 p8).

The intention is to raise standards so that pupils are better able to access the next stage of their education. The current expectation that primary pupils achieve level 4 in English and mathematics do not equate to 'secondary readiness.' In 2012, fewer than half the pupils who just reached level 4 went on to achieve five GCSEs at 16, including English and mathematics. It could be argued that the problem might be at secondary school but the importance of primary schools cannot be underestimated. This is borne out by the fact that 70% of those with a good level 4 in these subjects achieve the five GCSE standard.

New end of key stage assessments will be introduced in summer 2016, after pupils have been taught the new National Curriculum for two years and both schools and pupils should prepare for this. These new National Curriculum tests will be more demanding to ensure that pupils are genuinely ready to succeed in secondary education. The aim is for 85% of pupils to be secondary-ready by the end of Key Stage 2. Therefore the aim should be that at least 85% of pupils are working at their expected grammar and punctuation age. However the document can also be used for progression, so a child starting Key Stage 2 at a higher stage, can be targeted to continue working at this level, while a child working at a lower stage will need a catch up programme to accelerate progress.

Using the progression in grammar grids

Take time to look through the grids. What are the implications in relation to your subject knowledge and pitch and expectation? At the end of each column is the terminology needed at that stage. Within the progression in grammar grids the following features are included:

- word level – where the emphasis is on improving vocabulary (e.g. using powerful verbs or adjectives)
- sentence structure – focuses on aspects such as varying sentence openers (e.g. using a range of conjunctions or complex sentences)
- text structure and organisation – looks at the flow of writing (e.g. through the use of pronouns or tense choices).

Teachers have found these grids useful, especially to help differentiation and set targets. For example the focus of the lesson might be to improve descriptive vocabulary; the teacher can look at what this looks like at a variety of stages. They have also found it easier to use and to give pupils constructive feedback from.

The grid is an indicator of expectations throughout a school. It should be used as a teaching tool initially, to identify success criteria, as an aid to differentiation and setting targets. A number of case studies of children's work are explored in Chapter 8, looking at progression and what the child needs to be taught next.

Subject knowledge

If I had to go and teach, for example, parts of the plant to a Year 5 class tomorrow, I would need to look up the details in advance: I always forget which is the anther or filament. It is similar with grammar, sometimes you will want to check the terminology and look at examples of how it is used. With practice, knowledge does become embedded. A glossary is included at the back of this book which can be used to further support the glossary within the new English curriculum and that published in support of the *English grammar, punctuation and spelling test*.

Test yourself

Some schools have used the published example grammar tests with staff, particularly level 6, to identify grammatical terms teachers are less familiar with and then support staff accordingly. Otherwise you might want to try the following challenge, with teachers discussing the words in italics.

Develop the following simple sentence: 'The dog ran after the cat.' – the result might be one finished sentence or teachers may choose to return to the original simple sentence at some stage:

- use a more *powerful verb*
- use a *noun phrase* to tell us more about the *subject* of the sentence
- add a subordinate clause to make a *complex sentence*
- add a *fronted adverbial*
- use *semi-colons* for a complex list, where the dog chases three animals.

With new initiatives, new terminology may be used for concepts you are already familiar with. For example, you might be familiar with the term 'adverbial phrase', which describes when, where or how something happens. However the 2014 National Curriculum refers to 'fronted adverbials'. This just means the phrase comes at the start of the sentence, as in the example given below.

One possible answer to the challenge: 'As the sun set, while his owner returned home, the white and tan spaniel with wagging tail chased the small squeaking mouse; the terrified cat; and the squawking duck.'

Definitions of terms can be found in the Glossary, page 95.

5
Teach: Writing workshops and modelled writing

'If you do three things only when you teach writing, make sure it is these: model, model and model some more.'

Megan Sloan

Key concept

We saw in Chapter 2, how grammar is best taught in context within children's everyday writing. The key method of doing so is through a writing workshop approach, where modelled writing is a key element. Within a writing workshop approach the teacher acts as a writing professional and peer coach, guiding authors as they explore their craft. Instead of spending the majority of time on spelling tests, grammar worksheets, handwriting practice, and other isolated skills, modelled writing is designed to emphasise the act of writing itself. Within this process, the grammar and punctuation identified is explicitly taught.

In this chapter you will:

- **develop the ability to support children when investigating grammatical rules and conventions**
- **understand how to deconstruct a text to analyse grammatical features**
- **learn how to teach grammar and punctuation through explicit teaching and modelling**

Writing workshops and the 2014 curriculum

This approach is built into the 2014 National Curriculum, where children are expected to work through the process of writing. So in Years 3 and 4 pupils are expected to plan their writing by discussing writing similar to their own. They then draft their ideas, composing and rehearsing sentences orally, organising paragraphs and considering settings, characters and plot in narratives and organisational devices in non-narrative. Finally they should evaluate, edit and proofread their work.

When modelling, the teacher writes, using success criteria identified previously while thinking aloud and explaining choices being made. There should normally be a specific focus to concentrate on taken from the 2014 curriculum, with the teacher choosing to work at word, sentence or text level, though this doesn't preclude the teaching of other points if they arise.

Explicitly teaching the key aspects of grammar and punctuation

Before modelling, you need to first explain and teach the aspect of grammar or punctuation you are looking at. Ideally this should be a short activity. Remember you will be demonstrating the skill during text deconstruction and modelling, and there will be further opportunities to practise and apply skills learnt later. If you need to spend longer on this do so, but try to avoid going down the route of endless worksheets and decontextualised activities.

Try to set aside at least two, 15 minute sessions a week, to directly teach or practise the knowledge and skills you are focussing on. Many of the practise games in Chapter 6 are suitable for this but you might want the children to first investigate the aspect of grammar or punctuation you are looking at.

Grammar and punctuation investigation

If children investigate a concept first, they are more likely to remember it. Research shows it doesn't matter if all the children don't get to the answer themselves. At some stage you will need to stop the class and clearly explain the concept. However the fact that they were investigating for themselves, makes the final answer more meaningful; there is an 'aha' moment when the penny does finally drop.

To start the investigation, give children a text with the part of speech or punctuation you are looking for highlighted. This might well be part of text deconstruction, as described below, but another text can be used. The children then investigate what the words or marks have in common, e.g.

> The dwarf, with his long red fiery beard, **led** the way while intensely **studying** an ancient leather scroll. Like a nervous rat, his eyes **darted** left to right, **making sure** no one else **could see**. This was no **ordinary** scroll: he would guard it with his life if he **had to**. In his hands, it was an ancient dwarf map, the only one of its kind; a map that **could take** them through the caverns of the dwarf king, to their destination – the treasure crypts of the terrifying mountain dragon.

For the text above a number of investigations could be set up. I have highlighted the verbs for children to investigate what these words have in common. I have deliberately emboldened one word that is not a verb, to see if they can spot it (ordinary). There is a lot to unpick here as some verbs are in the past tense but some are in the present tense continuous (e.g. studying) and auxillary verbs, such as **could** are included. This would form part of your differentiation, depending on the ability of the children. You can always use a simpler text.

Other investigations could be set up through highlighting different aspects of grammar and punctuation. For example, with the above text, children might look at the use of commas. Again this is quite a difficult concept, as children would need to look at grammatical boundaries and at least know what a complex sentence is. The main point is not to try and explain everything at once. Let children investigate and get the basics. Through the practise games and application the concept can be developed further.

Identify, create and change

Another useful technique to teach the knowledge and skills needed is using the identify, create and change sequence. This technique is also used within Chapter 6, as many of the games and activities are suitable for explicitly teaching and recapping on the knowledge and skills needed.

The first step is for the children to identify the grammar or punctuation feature you are teaching. So with complex sentences, a number of sentences can be provided for children to identify as simple, compound or complex. They then might create their own complex sentence based on a picture or activity. Finally, sentences might be provided for children to make complex, through adding a clause and subordinating conjunction.

This is a vital step within the teaching sequence. Often I have discussed a child's target where they are asked to use complex sentences. However they can't identify one or explain how they are created. Once targets are given the knowledge needed must be explicitly taught before it can be applied.

Modelling writing

I am often asked to demonstrate lessons using modelled writing. When I do so teachers are surprised by how much grammatical language I use but always respond positively. The grammar does not get in the way of the learning and is not a test for the children. Rather, I am using the correct terminology so children become familiar with it. Within this process skills are explicitly taught. The diagram below, from the Primary Framework (2007), shows the three main methods used when modelling writing.

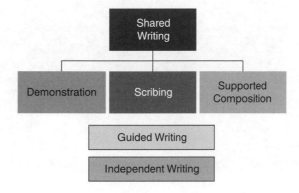

Demonstration writing

The teacher writes using 'think alouds' to show the choices they are making. When modelling, it is first important to decide on either:

- the mood for fiction, e.g. to build tension or reflect on what has happened
- the purpose for non-fiction e.g. to persuade or inform.

This will often influence the success criteria, which are identified through text deconstruction and using the progression in grammar grids (Appendix 1), so that the modelling matches the ability of the children.

Scribing

Through questioning and discussion the children compose aloud, while the teacher writes their ideas.

Supported composition

With the whole class or a group of children this typically involves the children writing the next sentence on whiteboards. The teacher then uses one of these to discuss and develop. With an individual, it consists of the teacher working alongside and writing with the child, making decisions about what the child can do independently and how best to support them.

The teacher does not just use one of these techniques in a session but rather moves from one to the other. The process needs to be interactive, the children would become bored if they were expected to sit quietly while the teacher demonstrates. Instead the teacher might demonstrate writing a sentence, then ask for ideas and finally the children in pairs compose a sentence on whiteboards to share. There is no formula and teachers need to be flexible. Two examples of modelled writing are given below.

Modelled writing based on an illustration from *Where the Wild Things Are*

Using an illustration from a favourite book as a basis for writing always works well. It is important that books are enjoyed for their own sake first and discussed. Once you start modelling writing, the first decision is to decide on the purpose of the writing. What are you trying to do?

Looking at this illustration from *Where the Wild Things Are* by Maurice Sendak (Red Fox 1963), the first thing we notice is that the picture has a magical quality and I want to get that into my writing. The next consideration is to model at a level just above where the children are at. In this example, I am modelling at a punctuation and grammar age of 7.5 years (a secure level 2) and this helped me decide my success criteria based upon the PoS from the 2014 National Curriculum for English and the progression in grammar grids (Appendix 1). Pupils should be taught to:

- use adjectives and expanded noun phrases for description and specification (e.g. the blue butterfly, the man in the moon)
- use subordination (using when, if, that or because) and co-ordination (using or, and, but).

Next, with the children, identify key things you are going to write about. So in the illustration we can see the moon, two monsters and Max. Now I am ready to start modelling but having the right tools for the job are important. Children need to actually see the process of writing, with the teacher putting pen to paper and for this a flipchart is ideal. You might want to first explicitly recap on the knowledge needed through using one of the short sentence games. So for example you might give three sentences for children to combine using 'and', 'but', 'so' or 'yet'. The extract in the box shows what the process might look like.

Teacher:	"Now how should I start my writing? I think I will start by describing the setting, where Max is. I want to describe the scene just before Max meets the monsters. The moon is in the sky and the stars are sparkling. So how might I start? I could start with an adverbial phrase for where e.g. 'Under the moonlit sky…'"
Sentence 1:	I demonstrate and write on the board, 'Under the moonlit sky, Max came upon the monsters.'
Teacher:	"Now I want to describe one of the monsters just before the picture displayed? These aren't the timid creatures in the picture. These are big, scary monsters that look like they might attack Max. Lets' work together on this and try to describe the monster. How might I describe the creature using an adjective or noun phrase? "
Sentence 2:	The children come up with a number of adjectives to describe the monster including scary, large horned and yellow eyed. We decide on: 'The large horned, yellow eyed monster, stared at Max and…' I give children time to add another clause. They complete the sentence referring to the original story, '…and roared its terrible roar.'
Teacher:	"Let's describe what is happening in the picture now. The monsters are being calmed by Max. Turn to your partner and describe two or three things that you can see happening?"
Sentence 3:	The pupils come up with a number of ideas and I discuss how these might be joined using a compound conjunction, 'and', 'but', or 'so'. The children make suggestions and I scribe, 'Max walked up to the beasts and tamed them with a magic stare.'
Teacher:	"Finally I want you to describe what happens to the other monster. On your whiteboards describe the monster and what it does. Make a compound sentence using the conjunction 'so', 'yet' or 'but'.
Sentence 4:	The final sentence from a child is chosen and worked upon. I write on the board, 'The smaller monster flung itself to the ground so ending the battle.'

This might be sufficient for the stage the children are at but if I wanted to challenge the children I could return to the text and look at how we might amend and vary the sentence starters. For example I could have made sentence three more complex by starting with when: When Max walked up to the beasts, he tamed them with a magic stare. The grammar arises naturally from the writing and can be discussed as it arises, without getting in way of the process of writing itself.

Text deconstruction and modelled writing based on *The Lost Happy Endings*

Often teachers struggle initially with modelling writing but through looking at a text first, gain in confidence. Just as the children magpie ideas and use a text as a starting point for writing, so can the teacher. This example uses one of my favourite books *The Lost Happy Endings* by Carol Ann Duffy and Jane Ray (Bloomsbury 2008). It is important it is read and appreciated for its own sake first. This matches the aims of the 2014 National Curriculum, so in Year 2 pupils should be taught to develop pleasure in reading and listen to discuss and express their views. A lesson was spent prior to modelling to explore what the pupils liked about the book and any patterns or puzzles were identified.

Text deconstruction

An extract from the text was displayed and the children were asked what impact the writer was trying to create. As with the first example, it is best to establish the purpose of the writing at the start. The mood here is frightening and mysterious and the author is trying to hide what's about to happen. A range of sentences are used, some short for dramatic impact and some long to help build a picture of what is happening. After this the text was annotated with the children as shown below.

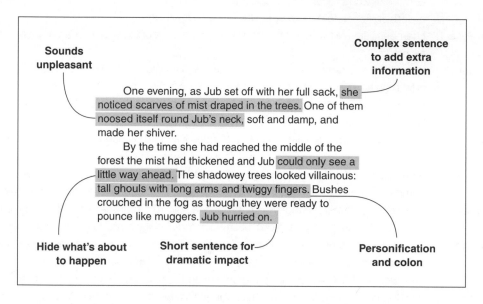

This deconstruction of the text then became the basis for writing and the identification of success criteria. Shirley Clarke (2003) suggests that success criteria should be known by the teacher first but developed with the children. Using the 2014 National Curriculum and progression in grammar grids (Appendix 1) the teacher might identify the following:

In narratives, describe settings, characters and atmosphere (taken from the Year 5 PoS):

- Use adverbials and expanded noun phrases to make the writing frightening and mysterious
- Experiment with complex sentences to clarify relationships in time and place. (Punctuation and grammar age 10 – level 4b)

These would then be developed in collaboration with the children. At this stage, as a teacher, you might be ready to model but first you might want to teach the skill as explained above using the identify, create and change sequence referred to on page 31. This will depend on where you are within the writing process and might well have been taught in a previous lesson. Then you may want to discuss with the children the text you are using to model from and the grammar involved.

Teacher: "Let's start by looking at the opening sentence and consider what it does. 'One evening, as Jub set off with her full sack, she noticed scarves of mist draped in the trees.' I love this sentence, the way the mist is draped in the trees. The sentence starts with an adverbial phrase for where, followed by a subordinate clause and finally the main clause."

Subject knowledge

There is a lot to explore with children here and these are all elements that children are expected to identify and use within the English grammar, punctuation and spelling test.

Adverbial phrases commonly describe who, where or when. So in the original sentence 'One evening,' is an adverbial phrase for when.

Complex sentences contain the main clause and a subordinate clause, giving the reader extra information. Most subordinate clauses will begin with a subordinate conjunction and will contain both a subject and a verb. This combination of words will not form a complete sentence, instead it will make a reader want additional information to finish the thought. So in our sentence the clause – 'as Jub set off with her full sack,' does not make sense in its own right but let's us know what Jub was doing.

Modelled writing

Once you have identified the grammar you are studying you are ready to teach and then model writing. You will need to decide what is the main focus of the session. Is it fronted adverbials or complex sentences? If it is the latter, two or three sentences can be given for children to combine, as explained in the next chapter. We are then ready to model writing. In the example below I look at both aspects as this is a more able group. I also look at the use of the colon, though in reality this would probably be done in a separate session. We decide to change the setting to a city.

Teacher:	"Now I want to start like the original did, with an adverbial phrase, and complex sentence." The original is displayed. 'One evening, as Jub set off with her full sack, she noticed scarves of mist draped in the trees.' "I want you to picture Jub in the city, with rushing traffic and tall buildings. So let's start with an adverbial for when."
Sentence 1:	Suggestions are taken from the class including: 'at the stroke of midnight;' 'just after rush hour;' and 'late at night'. I write on board the fronted adverbial, 'Just after rush hour…' We next want to write about what she noticed. What might she have seen in the city? Suggestions include: people rushing around, fumes coming from the subway and flying pigeons overhead. Our completed sentence became: 'Just after rush hour, as Jub set off with her full sack, she noticed fumes of smoke coming from the subway.' We then move onto the next sentence.
Teacher:	"I particularly liked the way the original text used personification, saying the trees looked villainous followed by a colon and supporting phrase to elaborate. What feeling could we give to those skyscrapers?"
Sentence 2:	The children suggested they were evil, murderous and haunting. Murderous was chosen and then we looked at describing the windows and doors of the tower blocks. The completed sentence became: 'The skyscrapers looked murderous: glittering eyes and gaping mouths.'
Teacher:	"Now I want the witch to appear on the scene but I don't want to start my sentence with the noun, Jub. I also want to describe the witch. What extra information could I give to make a more interesting sentence? Let's try starting with a continuous verb using an 'ing' verb.

Sentence 3: 'Cackling loudly,' is suggested and then the children complete the sentence in pairs and one is chosen to work on together. I scribe: 'Cackling loudly, the evil witch, with large hooked nose and piercing eyes, emerged through the smoke. Her breath smelt foul and small spiders crawled in her hair.'

Sentence 4: A simple, final short sentence is chosen: 'Jub froze.'

Once the demonstration is complete, children write their own version using the success criteria identified. For the independent writing phase you might want to give the children more choice in the direction of their writing. The important point is that they apply the skills taught, such as using complex sentences to add interesting details. You might suggest that they keep within the theme of a traditional story but change one aspect. For example the main character might have something different that makes people happy rather than a happy ending, a pet perhaps or fabulous paintings.

The explicit teaching of punctuation and application through modelled writing

The process again starts with a book and exploring how professional authors use the form of punctuation chosen. For example with speech, a text is explored and success criteria identified such as:

- Put inverted commas around what is actually said.
- Punctuate both within the speech marks and at the end of the sentence.
- Use a range of verbs other than 'said' e.g. sniggered, mumbled or wailed.
- Use infill to further develop your character. This is where you explain what the character is doing while they talk.
- Most importantly don't overuse: make sure speech is used in a way that develops the characters or plot.

The skill is then explicitly taught but within the context of the writing being worked on. One good technique is to use the idea of a speech sandwich: the bread at either end is the speech marks, the filling the speech and the spread the punctuation, which goes inside the sandwich. Then at the end, add who said it and what they were doing if appropriate.

For example: 'This should do for tonight,' the soldier whispered, as he pointed to an alcove in the rock wall.

The children then apply the technique within their own writing. Further aspects of speech, such as placing who said it at the start of the sentence or within the speech can be developed in subsequent lessons, practice sessions or within guided writing. Other aspects of punctuation such as the use of semi-colons, or commas in a list, can be taught in a similar way.

As the children write independently, the teacher should sit with a group for guided writing. Guided writing provides children with a structured opportunity to practise skills taught and can be seen as an interim step between working with the whole class and independent writing. This technique is explored further in Chapter 7.

6
Practise: Word level games and activities

'Do not keep children to their studies by compulsion but by play.'

Plato

Key concept

Once grammar has been taught through identification in reading, explicit teaching and modelled writing, it needs to be practised and applied. We have seen how the research shows grammar is best taught in context, within the child's own writing. However skills taught do need to be practised, so the idea of little and often works well. Also in these sessions children will be presented with questions that are similar to those used in the *English grammar, punctuation and spelling test*. It is important that children do experience the types of questions they will have to answer at the end of Year 2 and Year 6.

In this chapter you will:

* **develop your knowledge of a range of grammar games and activities**
* **know how audience and purpose help develop the vocabulary pupils use, through activities such as the mood game**
* **be able to use sentence combining, parts of speech and other activities to support sentence development**
* **learn how to support children with text cohesion and organisation**

Planning for grammar games and activities

When first introducing a new activity you might initially need more time but once introduced, aim to practise the game on a regular basis in short sessions of between five to 15 minutes. With an overcrowded curriculum, one of the problems teachers face is trying to fit everything in. I would suggest at least two sessions a week, which might be as a starter within the main literacy lesson, or at some other point in the timetable. The activities below can also be used as teach sessions before modelling writing.

Ofsted have identified that planning is often too complicated in schools. While it is recognised teachers should not have to plan in detail for such short sessions, it is important with all activities that they are objective-led and match the needs of the children. The learning intention should be shared, so that there is a clear focus for both the teacher and children to evaluate work against. The grammar focus might relate to the main part of the lesson, for example if you are working on describing a setting you could focus on expanded noun phrases. At other times you will want to respond to common errors children are making.

When the games are being played it should be the intention that some writing will happen, for example, children might write their favourite sentence, not necessarily every one spoken and practised with a partner. Presentation is important and good quality, lined whiteboards can work well. However, do expect some of the writing to go into books, so that there is a more permanent record. Most of the activities are intended to be collaborative, so encourage lots of discussion about language and the changes made.

At the start of each of the sections at word, sentence and text level there is a possible planning format. Learning intentions are at the top, taken from the 2014 National Curriculum for English, followed by relevant progression in grammar statements which can be used to help generate success criteria. The games and activities are explained and these can be played as a whole class or in groups. These are examples and as such can be adapted so that they become part of the teacher's repertoire. For each game, tips are given on how to create your own version.

Below is a simplified format that can be adopted when planning text level games and activities.

Year 1 / 2 Learning intention: Y2 (2014 National Curriculum) • discuss favourite words and phrases • use expanded noun phrase	Learning intention: Y3/4 (2014 National Curriculum) • include a varied and rich vocabulary • use vocabulary for effect • use imaginative vocabulary • use fronted adverbials • choose nouns appropriately	Learning intention Y5/6 (2014 National Curriculum) • select appropriate grammar and vocabulary, understanding how such choices can change and enhance meaning
Example outcomes		

Year 2 *(PaG age 7.5 – level 2)*	Year 3/4 *(PaG age 8.5 – level 3)*	Year 5 *(PaG age 10 – level 4)*	Year 6 *(PaG age 11.5 – level 5)*
Adverbs tell the reader when, where and how things happen. Use adjectives and simple expanded noun phrases for description (e.g. the boy in the blue jeans).	Use expanded **noun phrases** to add interest and detail (e.g. *the spooky house on the corner*). Use adverbial phrases (including fronted adverbials) to give clarity (e.g. At midnight . . .).	Indicating degrees of possibility using adverbs (e.g. perhaps, surely) or modal verbs (e.g. might, should, will, must). Use stylistic devices, (e.g. simile – the dragon stared with eyes of ice).	Additional words and phrases contribute to shades of meaning e.g. Joe was_____ when his cat went missing. [sad, depressed, heartbroken]). Use expanded noun phrases to convey complicated information concisely (e.g. The rubbish lying at the bottom of the canal . . .).

Possible games				
The mood game	VAK game	Cloze procedure	Zone of relevance	Improve the sentence
Word overload	Definitions	Shopping list	Description game	Word match
Expand a sentence				

Differentiation	Key questions
Support – Consider giving key vocabulary to use.	Where did you get your ideas from? (Refer to reading, films and experiences.)
Extension – Once children have acquired a skill let them spend time applying it within their own writing.	What changes did you make?
	Is there a different word you could you use?
	Does this help me to picture the scene?

Words level games

'There is something about words. In expert hands, manipulated deftly, they take you prisoner. Wind themselves around your limbs like spider silk, and when you are so enthralled you cannot move, they pierce your skin, enter your blood, numb your thoughts. Inside you they work their magic.'

— Diane Setterfield, *The Thirteenth Tale*

The mood game

Vocabulary development is a key component of the 2014 National Curriculum. 'Pupils' acquisition and command of vocabulary are key to their learning and progress across the whole curriculum,' (*The National Curriculum in England Key stages 1 and 2 framework document p11* (Department for Education 2013).

This game illustrates just how important audience and purpose are to this development. Children are given a dull text and asked to improve it to match a certain mood or purpose. I find this activity always

Taylor walked through the streets. He looked round. He saw a building. He went inside. He met a man who looked at him with eyes. He ran away.	Rewrite as a horror story or spy thriller.
Taylor walked through the woods. He looked round. He met a witch (or a dwarf or elf). It had eyes and a nose. The witch said . . . Taylor moved away.	Rewrite as a fantasy or traditional tale.
Taylor sailed on a boat. The weather was rainy. Another boat came along. People jumped on board. There was a fight. Taylor was captured.	Rewrite as a pirate adventure or Famous Five Adventure.
Taylor says he shouldn't do so much homework. He likes to play out. He learns at school. Mr Jones thinks he should do lots of homework. It helps him.	Rewrite as a persuasive piece of writing or newspaper report.

generates lots of collaboration and laughter. If children were just asked to add adjectives or improve the verbs, the result would be far less exciting.

Other scenarios can be written for children to improve by changing the setting, characters and genre. As with all the games suggested, an element of competiveness can be introduced by using a simple scoring system. This activity should not just be about adding adjectives. At the end ask children to share and evaluate a favourite sentence.

The VAK game

In this game language created can be discussed and in relation to the *English grammar, punctuation and spelling test*, the use of the term noun phrase can be introduced or consolidated.

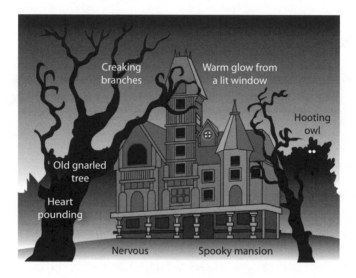

Children are asked to generate words or phrases to go along with a picture using the following prompts:

- **V = visual:** 'turn the colours up' and talk with a partner about what you **see**
- **A = auditory:** 'turn the sound up' and describe what you can **hear**
- **K = kinaesthetic:** 'jump in' to the picture describe what you can **feel** both physically and emotionally

Once completed, share words and phrases generated and allow children to 'magpie': adding any that they like to their own list. A good bank of images is needed, which you can collect from picture books, the internet, topic or cross curricular work. If there is time, the children can then generate sentences which can be read out and shared with the class, though you might want to do this in a later session. With the idea above for example, the following sentence might be generated: 'With my heart pounding I nervously approached the spooky mansion. Branches creaked and an owl hooted from the old gnarled tree. At the top of the house, the warm glow from a lit window beckoned me on.' Subject knowledge can be made explicit by asking pupils to identify their favourite noun phrase.

Cloze procedure

Children are given a sentence and asked to fill in the missing words. Sentences can be taken from a book you are using with the class, either fiction or non-fiction. The level of text can easily be differentiated through using a book at the child's reading level.

The terrifying wolf pounced suddenly on her prey, while the rest of the hungry pack looked on. However the arctic hare was too quick and scurried away into its warm burrow.

Certain words can be omitted and children asked to fill in possible answers. You might want to look at one word class at a time. For example, all the adjectives have been omitted below.

The _____ wolf pounced suddenly on her prey, while the rest of the _____ pack looked on. However the _____ hare was too quick and scurried away into its _____ burrow.

Another version of the game is to ask children to replace words. In the version below, children have to think of alternative adverbs to use for those underlined.

The wolf pounced <u>suddenly</u> on her prey, while the rest of the pack looked on. <u>Quickly</u> the arctic hare scurried away.

Zone of relevance

With all the word level games, it is important to remember we are trying to develop vocabulary. Once words and phrases have been generated, it is important that they are shared and discussed. Pie Corbett uses the term 'magpieing', where children take words from their reading or each other, to use in their own writing. Children need to understand this is not copying but something all writers do. If the games are played in pairs, children can use the words to create their own zone of relevance in groups.

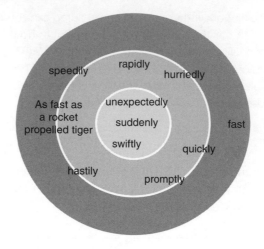

The original word is placed in the centre, I have chosen **suddenly.** Children write synonyms on sticky notes, at this stage all options are equally valid and shared as a class. Next a sentence is given and children decide which words work best. The point is not that any of the children's words are wrong, but that certain ones work better in this context. So for the example, 'The wolf pounced suddenly . . .', words that work less well are placed on the outside, while words that work best go towards the centre. The teacher can then discuss the words generated, which can be displayed or added to examples using an interactive whiteboard for future reference. Phrases can be used, though the metaphor used in the above example does not work particularly well.

Improve the sentence

Start with a boring sentence and then work your way through the instructions below. For example you might start with a dull sentence such as: 'The mouse went down the path.' When introducing this for the first time you might only do the first few, but as children get more competent, expect to get further down the list. When working on vocabulary it is always about quality rather than speed.

- Add an adjective e.g. 'The timid mouse'.

- Replace the verb with a more powerful one e.g. 'The timid mouse slunk down the path.'

- Add an adverb e.g. 'Hesitantly the timid mouse slunk down the path.'

- Use a connective and a comma e.g. 'The timid mouse slunk down the path, while the monster looked on.'

- Reorder the words e.g. 'The monster looked on hungrily, while the timid mouse slunk down the path.'

- Drop in a clause e.g. 'The timid mouse, who had never before been out without his mother, slunk down the path.'

- Add a simile e.g. 'The timid mouse, like a fly caught in a web, slunk down the path while the monster prepared to pounce.'

This activity is ideal to develop pupil's knowledge of word classes in preparation for the requirements of the 2014 National Curriculum for English and the *English grammar, punctuation and spelling test*.

Word overload

Once taught a skill, it is common for children to overuse it. In this game, children identify which words can be omitted and a more specific noun might be considered.

> In the large, green, branching, old tree the extremely hungry, green and red caterpillar munched the delicate, new, green leaves. The busy, black and yellow bumble bee flew hurriedly, quickly and suddenly past. The yellow beaked bird with black beady eyes, deep brown feathers and large wings got ready to pounce.

Definitions

Give the children a word to define, discuss suggestions and agree on the best definition. Children then discuss the word thinking about who was doing it, where, when, how and why? They then make a sentence containing the word.

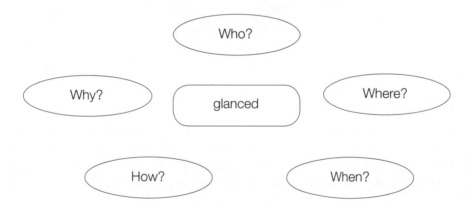

For example, 'Not wanting to attract attention, the robber glanced quickly at the diamonds on the table'.

Try this approach with other words taken from children's reading or try the following words: lingered, crawled, approached, chased, giggled, perched and snatched.

Shopping lists: common nouns

This is a simple memory game, where you start with a short list of items and children add further words. Traditionally this starts with 'I went to the shops and bought an apple', with children adding extra words when it's their turn. It can also be used to explore a topic for example: I went to India and bought a silk sari, golden saffron and a king cobra.

Describing game

Give children a word or picture, such as a kitten or old lady's face for children to generate adjectives to describe. So with the illustration below, basic nouns are given and children can be asked to expand using adjectives or a noun phrase e.g. they might describe the old lady's 'paper-thin skin, wrinkled with time' or her 'piercing blue eyes which reflect the intelligence of her age'.

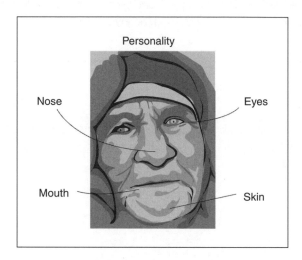

Word match

Pupils draw an object or write a word which they then pass to their partner. They then have a set time to write a number of adjectives that match the picture, e.g. the drawing of a tree might be matched to gigantic, oak, apple, hollow, etc. This game can also be played using verbs and adverbs, which once matched can be acted out for the class to guess e.g. jump – slowly, cautiously, quickly.

Expand a sentence

Start with a simple sentence and the children expand the noun phrase and verb chain, e.g.

The boy	swam.
The small boy	swam quickly.
The small boy, without any thought for his own safety	swam quickly to save the dog.

With this activity, once children have started using the technique, you can introduce a matrix to look at the grammatical structures in more detail. So, for noun phrases the following can be used:

Determiner	Adjective	Noun	Embedded clause	Verb	Adverb
The	fierce	tiger,	with no thought of danger	jumped	suddenly
Some	noisy	children	who were playing outside	laughed	hysterically
The	Oak	tree	that had stood for years	swayed	precariously

To start, part of the matrix can be omitted and then children can go on to create their own versions.

Determiner	Adjective	Noun	Embedded clause	Verb	Adverb
The		tiger	with no thought of danger	jumped	
Some	noisy	children		laughed	
The		tree		swayed	

Practise: Sentence structure games and activities

'The teaching of sentence combining, is one of probably a number of methods, that is effective.'

(p39). Andrews R, et al (2004),

Key concept

If children play with and manipulate sentences their writing, and grammar and punctuation will improve.

Planning for sentence games

Below is a simplified format that can be adapted when planning sentence games and activities.

Learning intention Y2	Learning intention: Y3/4	Learning intention: Y5/6
• use both familiar and new punctuation correctly including full stops, capital letters, exclamation marks, question marks and commas for lists	• extend the range of sentences with more than one clause by using a wider range of conjunctions, e.g. when, if, because, although	• propose changes to grammar, vocabulary and punctuation to enhance effects and clarify meaning

Example outcomes			
Year 2 *(PaG age 7 – level 2)*	**Year 3/4** *(PaG age 8.5 – level 3)*	**Year 5** *(PaG age 10.5 – level 4)*	**Year 6** *(PaG age 11.5 – level 5)*
Use sentences with different forms: statement, question, exclamation, command. Clauses joined in compound sentences using and, but, so, or.	Use a variety of sentence openings to express time and cause, using: • conjunctions (e.g. when, before, after, while) • adverbs (e.g. then, next, soon, so) • prepositions (e.g. before, after, during, in, because of). Use some complex sentences e.g. After running for the bus, I collapsed on the seat.	Continue to experiment with complex sentences to clarify relationships in time and place. Variety in subordinating connectives: because, if, which (because the rain can damage their skin. . . which was strange. . . If she could . . .). Experiment with the position of subordinate clauses to create effect Use relative clauses beginning with who, which, where, why, or whose.	Variety in sentence length, structure and subject to help expand ideas, convey key issues/facts or provide emphasis, detail and description. A range of subordinate connectives (while, until, despite) with possible use of several subordinate clauses to aid economy of expression ('While under my roof, you will obey my rules, which are clearly displayed.').

Possible games

Sentence building game   Sentence combining   Consequences   Complex sentence game

Model sentences   Free writing   Stolen punctuation   Continue the sentence

Photo match   The if game

Differentiation	**Key questions**
Support – Give children frames and model sentences. Extension – Once children have acquired a skill let them spend time applying it within their own writing.	Is the meaning clear for the reader? Do I need more information? Have you used a variety of sentence lengths? How can we start this sentence in a different way?

Sentence building game

Copy the sheets in Appendix 2 (page 91) and then make cards in the various colours indicated by copying onto coloured card.

Within the 2014 National Curriculum for English and as part of the *English grammar, punctuation and spelling test* pupils are expected to identify words based on the eight parts of speech: the verb, noun, pronoun, adjective, adverb, preposition, conjunction and determiner. This game is a great fun way to get children to recognise each part. It takes a while to set up at first, but once pupils get used to sorting out the cards it becomes relatively quick. Team points can be given to encourage being first ready, the quickest sentence, etc. Though there are potentially eight sets of cards, prepositions and pronouns aren't always used. So if played in a team of six, each person gets one set of cards. They lay the cards out in front of them so others can see and discuss the choices made. Then follow the instructions below, the child with the part of speech referred to e.g. the noun or adjective, will lay down their card to form a joint sentence with the group:

- Make a simple sentence using just three cards. You will find you have used a blue card (noun), a red card (verb) and a determiner (e.g. the, a or an). These are the standard colours used for parts of speech.

- Now add an adjective (green card). Can you change the position of the adjective without changing the meaning? (The answer is no!)

- Now add an adverb (yellow). Can you change its position? The answer is yes – the adverb can normally go at the beginning, middle or end of a sentence. Point out adverbs often end in -ly and they are useful to start sentences with.

- Keep the sentence you have made and now add another sentence beneath.

- Can you join the two sentences together using one of the conjunctions (pale yellow).

- Finally add the punctuation cards. Where might a comma go? You might also investigate adding a preposition or pronoun.

It is easy to make further sets of your own cards, start with five or six sentences first to mix up, rather than using random words. Sets for different themes work well, such as 'The Ancient Greeks' with nouns like Heracles (Hercules in Roman).

Once children have become used to the parts of speech and their respective colours a number of related activities can be introduced. Try putting blank A4 colour sheets up that follow the parts of speech colours. Children then can be asked to suggest words relating to the text they are writing. So if they are writing the dilemma to a story they might be asked for nouns for the blue sheet, such as 'monster' or 'dragon'. Powerful verbs are then written on a red sheet such as 'pounced' and 'roared'. On the green sheet children might suggest adjectives such as 'frightening' and 'armoured', and on the yellow sheet adverbs like 'immediately' and 'ferociously'. These then can be used to create sentences. Ask which word would make the best opening to the sentence e.g. Ferociously the armoured dragon pounced on its prey.

Sentence combining

When looking at the research in Chapter 2, we saw the potential of sentence combining as an alternative to traditional formal grammar. It gives children the opportunity to practise, play with, and manipulate sentences, in a practical way. The aim is not to produce longer sentences but to develop more effective ones. There is no correct answer but rather a number of possibilities. For example look at these three short sentences:

- The footballer was not tall.
- The footballer was not fast.
- The footballer was rather skilful.

Through cutting out unnecessary repetition and adding appropriate conjunctions, we can combine these three short sentences into a single, more coherent one, e.g., 'The footballer was neither tall nor fast, but was rather skilful'.

Below are a number of short sentences to get you started. For each I have indicated the grammatical change made:

Short sentences	Example answer
• The dog barked loudly. • The cat stood its ground.	The dog barked loudly but the cat stood its ground. (Uses a conjunction.)
• A cat strolled. • It didn't have a care. • It strolled onto the football pitch. • This happened before the match on Sunday afternoon.	Onto the football pitch, before the match on Sunday afternoon, a cat without a care strolled. (Starts with a preposition.)
• She was our teacher. • We were in Year 5. • She was great. • She had bright green eyes. • Her eyes were sparkling. • She told the most marvellous stories.	In Year 5 our teacher was great. She had bright green, sparkling eyes and told the best stories. (Fronted adverbial.)
• The man handed me a parcel. • He did this suspiciously. • The man had a long moustache. • The parcel was old and battered.	The old battered parcel was handed suspiciously to me, by the man with the long moustache. (Starts with the object to make a passive sentence.)
• I took the short cut home. • I went through the fields. • I thought I could save some time	Thinking I could save some time, I took the short cut home through the fields. (Continuous verb.) Through the fields I took a short cut; I thought I could save some time. (Uses a semi-colon.)
• It was cold. • Jack wore just his T-shirt. • He went outside.	Although it was cold, Jack went outside in just his T-shirt. (Complex sentence and subordinating connective.)
• The artist was the best in the city. • The artist painted. • He painted the most amazing landscapes.	The artist, who painted the most amazing landscapes, was the best in the city. (Uses a relative clause to embed a sentence.)

These ideas can be used to get started but after a while you will want to produce your own sets of short sentences to combine. One easy way of doing this is to use a book at the level the children are working at. Find a good sentence then simplify into a number of short, repetitive clauses that can be combined: e.g. 'Ottoline lived in Apartment 243, of the PW Huffledinck Tower, which everybody called the Pepperpot Building because it looked like one.' (from *Ottoline Goes to School*, Chris Riddell (Macmillan) p1). This can be simplified into:

- Ottoline lived in Apartment 243.
- The apartment was in the Huffledinck Tower.
- Everybody called the tower the Pepperpot Building.
- It looked like a pepperpot.

After combining a set of sentences in a variety of ways, take the time to discuss and evaluate combinations and to make the grammatical language explicit. Children might do this individually or in a group, reading their sentences out loud.

Basic questions to consider while evaluating their sentences include:

1 Meaning: have you kept the original meaning?
2 Clarity: can the sentence be easily understood?
3 Coherence: does the sentence flow?
4 Emphasis: are key words and phrases in the best order?
5 Concise: are there any words that need to be taken out?

The question game/consequences

These games let children practise a range of punctuation. In the question game, each child writes a question, folds the paper so that it is hidden and passes it on. On the paper they receive they write the answer to their own question. The consequences are supposed to be funny, e.g. 'What is your favourite food? Answer: Manchester.

Consequences is another popular game:

- First write a girl's name, fold the paper so it can't be seen and pass it on.
- On the paper you receive, write a boy's name beneath the fold. Don't look at what's written within the fold. Then pass the paper on.
- On the paper you next receive write where they met.

The game continues in this way, with the paper being passed after each instruction.

- Write what they did.
- Write what he said. Ensure your speech is punctuated correctly.
- Write what she said.
- Finally write the consequence or ending.

You might want to discourage using the names of children in the class. Using book or TV characters works well, e.g. 'Harry Potter and the Varmint met at a wedding. They played rugby under a silvery moon. He said, 'Do you like eating cheesy pizza?' She said, 'I like your woolly jumper, did you buy it from a sheep? They were then asked to leave the party for not singing loudly enough.'

Complex sentence game

This was always my favourite game from *Grammar for Writing* (DfEE 2000). Make up a set of cards as shown below. Write a complex sentence on the board, for example: 'As the boy hauled the heavy sack through the streets, the thief prepared to strike'.

Ask a child to choose one of the cards:

Change the verb	Change the subordinate clause	Move the subordinate clause
Replace the connective	Change the main clause	Change the subject in the main clause

In teams, the children then have to make the change suggested and discuss possible answers. Points can be given for the first to complete the task correctly or for writing the most exciting version, etc. This is an ideal game to practise manipulating sentences in preparation for the *English grammar, punctuation and spelling test*.

Model sentences

This activity is similar to that described when modelling writing but just one sentence is used as a starting point. It has the potential to really lift the standard of pupils' writing. First the children are given a sentence from a book and they discuss how it is organised and its rhythm. Then they are given a different character or setting (or let the children choose their own) to write a sentence in a similar style, as shown in the example below.

Once children have got the hang of this they can find sentences themselves while they are reading to manipulate and change.

Model sentence	Analysis	Character and setting	Example
The handle began to turn but there was no hand upon it. (*Leon and the Place Between*, Graham Baker-Smith 2008)	Compound sentence joined by a conjunction.	Trees in a forest.	The trees began to sway, yet there was no wind to move them.
Sam walked on, out of the town, towards the woods. (*Look What I've Got*, Anthony Browne, 1980)*	Starts with the main clause followed by two adverbial phrases for where.	A soldier marching to war	The soldier marched on, away from the village, towards the gun-fire.

Model sentence	Analysis	Character and setting	Example
Tall buildings scratched the sky, where the birds once sang. (Varmints, Helen Ward 2007)	Starts with a metaphor followed by a relative subordinate clause, starting with a pronoun.	Fish at a ship wreck.	Small fish swept the wreck, where the crew once laughed.
Inside the house her mother coughed, twice. (Cloud Tea Monkeys, Mal Peet and Elspeth Graham 2010)	Starts with an adverbial for where, followed by an action and a number.	A boy at the seaside.	At the seaside the boy patted the sand, three times.
Silver frost on barbed wire, strange tinsel, sparkled and winked. (The Christmas Truce, Carol Ann Duffy 2011)	Noun phrase followed by a metaphor and ending with two verbs.	A spider's web.	Silvery dew on a spider's web, sparkling diamonds, glistened and twinkled.

Free writing

In this activity, the child writes freely for a set period of time. You might want to start with just five minutes but challenge them to write for longer as their confidence builds. Children need opportunities to write about their own interests and a range of topics can be identified early in the year. The writing is like a flow of consciousness. Children can write about anything, but you might want to give them prompts to get started, e.g. describe where you are, tell me about your day; write about your family; imagine meeting a monster. Children should always have an audience in mind, so the piece should be read to a partner once completed. What they write doesn't have to be perfect nor complete. At the end of the session the child counts:

- the number of lines they wrote
- the number of full stops
- the number of capital letters
- the number of 'ands' or 'thens'.

This is then used as a target to try and improve next time they write. This isn't always about writing more but of writing with greater accuracy. Putting numbers on things can help motivate children and it certainly made a difference with Pam's writing, as seen in Chapter 8. Once the basics are established, children can also start to count and improve on the number of connectives, adverbials or adjectives, etc used.

Stolen punctuation

This can be played in two ways. You might want to just give a passage and let the children add the punctuation. The other way is to actually give them the missing punctuation in the correct order for them to add. So in the passage below the following punctuation is missing Cap, , . Cap, .

the dwarf with his long red fiery beard led the way while intensely studying an ancient leather scroll like a nervous rat his eyes darted left to right making sure no one else could see this was no ordinary scroll he would guard it with his life
Possible answer: The dwarf, with his long red fiery beard, led the way while intensely studying an ancient leather scroll. Like a nervous rat his eyes darted left to right, making sure no one else could see.

When discussing grammar it is important that children aren't given the impression there is always a right or wrong answer. The punctuation is used to aid the reader, so with the above example, the child might decide there is no need for the pause and comma after the dwarf.

Continue the sentence

This is a simple activity that develops skills pupils will need for the *English grammar, punctuation and spelling test*. The pupils are given a sentence to complete using a conjunction.

Sentence	Conjunctions
The squirrel jumped from the tree . . .	while, as, because
Many people stopped smoking . . .	so, consequently, although,

With both the activities above it is easy to create your own versions using sentences from a book as a starting point.

Photo match

Using visuals helps motivate children as writers and can be used with many of the above activities. In this game, the children choose from two or three photos and then decide on the genre of writing they want to use to match the picture. News items make a good source of pictures, like the pillow fight illustrated opposite or use the Internet to search for photos of the London Pillow Fight. A number of different questions can be used to scaffold the task.

Possible questions:

- Think about the style of writing you want to write, e.g. a recount or newspaper report.
- Write a title for your picture.
- Consider what you can see, hear and feel. Who are the characters? What is happening? When did it happen? Why did it happen?
- Think of words and phrases to match the picture.
- Create two sentences in the style of writing you have chosen.

The 'If game' (conditional sentences)

Children write an ending to a conditional sentence using a modal verb e.g.

- If my mum wins the lottery we might . . .
- If we have a heatwave we could . . .

Alternatively, display a list of modal verbs e.g. must, ought, could, may, might, would, should. Give a number of scenarios for children to write sentences about, e.g.

- Being a superhero, e.g. If I were a superhero I would . . .
- If gravity got turned off, e.g. If there was no gravity the cats would . . .

Text structure and cohesion activities and games

'Read a thousand books, and your words will flow like a river.'

Lisa See, *Snow Flower and the Secret Fan*

Key concept

Short games and activities can help improve the flow and structure of children' writing.

Below is a simplified format that can be adapted when planning test level games and activities.

Learning intention Y2	Learning intention Y3/4	Learning intention Y5/6
• cohesion • check their writing makes sense and that verbs to indicate time are used correctly and consistently	• propose changes to grammar and vocabulary to improve consistency • choose nouns or pronouns appropriately for clarity and cohesion	• use a wide range of devices to build cohesion within and across paragraphs • use further organisational and presentational devices to structure texts and guide the reader

Outcomes			
Year 2 *(PaG age 7.5 – level 2)* Some attempt to sequence ideas or events, e.g. by use of time related words; numbered points; headings, line breaks; use of pictures. Use of the continuous form of verbs in the present and past tense to mark actions in progress (e.g. she is drumming, he was shouting).	Year 3/4 *(PaG age 8.5 – level 3)* Within paragraphs / sections, some links between sentences e.g. use of pronouns or adverbials. Appropriate choice of pronoun or noun within a sentence to avoid ambiguity and repetition. Tense choice generally appropriate to task including some use of modals (can, will).	Year 5 *(PaG age 10 – level 4)* Use a wider range of sentence connectives to develop meaning e.g. if, when, rather than, although, however. Features of text type / genre are appropriate to the task, e.g. choice of tense / verb form; layout; formality. Link ideas across paragraphs using adverbials of time (e.g. later), place (e.g. nearby) and number (e.g. secondly).	Year 6 *(PaG age 11.5 – level 5)* A range of verb forms develops meaning and maintains appropriate tense choice. Use of the passive to affect the presentation of information in a sentence . Content is balanced and controlled with some effective selection and ordering of text to engage the reader.

Possible games
Boxing up   Clap the paragraph   Why the paragraph?   The connective game
Change the tense   Pronoun resolution   Overuse of nouns

Differentiation	**Key questions**
Support – Concentrate on imitation and learning basic stories / structures. Extension – Move on to invention once children have a good understanding of text types and story structure.	Does the writing flow? Are the words in the best order? Is it clear who the pronoun refers to? Does the writing make sense?

Verb tense game

Within the *English grammar, punctuation and spelling test* children are asked to circle the correct verb within a sentence. A good structure for teaching grammar is: identify, create and change.

1 Identify: Give children a number of sentences and let them identify if they are set in the past, present or future tense, e.g.

- John **plays** cricket at the weekend. (present)
- I **wrote** a poem about school. (past)
- The teacher **will read** to us. (future)

Remember, strictly speaking there is no future tense in English. The future tense is formed by adding the auxiliary verb 'will'.

2 Create: Give children verbs to create a sentence in the past, present and future tense, e.g. swim:

- Right now, Jack is swimming in a contest.
- Jack swam for the school team.
- Jack will swim tomorrow.

3 Change the tense: Give the children a text and ask them to change the tense e.g. change the story below into the past tense.

On the coach, Mrs Coggins sits with her three children. She takes in the views; the North Yorkshire Moors are wonderful, even on a grey day. One minute she is on the flat moors, with its bright purple heathers and steely grey skies and the next, in tree lined valleys with bright blue-green mosses and sparkling streams. 'I can see the sea,' Dan shouts. There is always a competition to see who is first to spot their destination and Dan usually wins.

Verb tense matrix

Learning a foreign language is of great benefit. When learning a foreign language it is usual to spend time on verb tenses and a similar approach can be used in English. This is of particular benefit for EAL children but also benefits disadvantaged pupils, who often hear incorrect language patterns at home.

Try a range of activities where children change the tense and subject. Below is an example of a matrix children can complete.

Present tense	Past tense	Future tense
I play	I played	I will play
		He will think
	They argue	

Present perfect game

As part of the New Curriculum, children in Year 3 and 4 are expected to learn the perfect present tense. This is a tense used to describe an action completed in the present using 'have' or 'has' e.g. Tom <u>has</u> finished his homework. This is particularly important for children with English as an additional language who do not have this form of grammar in their own language. It is often used where one event happens before another. Draw a timeline with two events such as swim and walk. Then ask children to create a sentence using have or has e.g. I have been swimming and next I will go for a walk.

Passive voice

Try using the structure 'identify, change and create' to practise this skill.

- Identify which is in the passive voice: John wrote the letter. The letter was written by John.
- Change the following to the passive voice: John answered all the questions.
- Create a passive sentence: give children pictures to create a sentence in both the active and passive voice e.g. a person eating ice cream or a boy kicking a ball.

Boxing up

Within the 2014 National Curriculum the importance of organising information and using paragraphs can be clearly seen in the PoS. While there is little about paragraphing within the *English grammar, punctuation and spelling test*, many of the questions do relate to text cohesion, through the use of verb tenses, pronouns, connectives, etc. Studying how this is done within and across paragraphs provides an ideal context to look at such aspects.

In Chapter 3, we looked at how learning to tell a bank of stories orally helps children internalise basic plots and language patterns which they then can use in their own writing. A useful strategy to develop this further is boxing up, a technique developed by Pie Corbett.

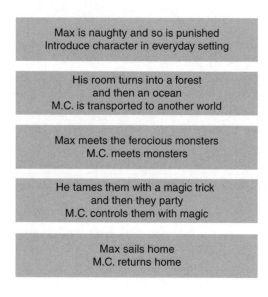

Max is naughty and so is punished
Introduce character in everyday setting

His room turns into a forest
and then an ocean
M.C. is transported to another world

Max meets the ferocious monsters
M.C. meets monsters

He tames them with a magic trick
and then they party
M.C. controls them with magic

Max sails home
M.C. returns home

(M.C. is a useful abbreviation for
main character.)

This activity relies on the fact that most stories follow a number of basic plots. First the story is broken down with the pupils, as shown on the top lines of each box above. Each box is discussed, in terms of what this represents in for the basic story structure and suggestions written down as shown as the second line of each box opposite. From this children can plan their own stories. In terms of grammar, this helps identify possible paragraphs and the features of each section can be discussed. For example:

- **The opening** introduces the character and setting and therefore needs to be descriptive.
- **The build-up** takes the character from the opening to where the main dilemma takes place. A journey is often involved and speech can be used to further develop characterisation.
- **The main dilemma** needs to build tension, which might be done through a mixture of short sentences and hiding what is about to happen.
- **The resolution** ensures all the loose ends are resolved.
- **The ending** is often reflective, referring back to the beginning.

Give children basic stories and a number of post-its. They then box up the story, discussing the main elements.

For example in Humpty Dumpty:

- The main character puts himself in a position of danger.
- As a result he has an accident.
- Others try to help him.
- The accident proves fatal.

Clap the paragraph

Show the pupils a short video, David Attenborough's wildlife films are ideal, and ask them to clap every time they think there is a new paragraph. The children will clap at different times but it is the discussion that is important, rather than correct answers. On another occasion, children can be asked to listen to the phrases used to start and end each section and how these link the paragraphs. The language used in the film needs to be of high quality.

Why the paragraph?

In shared or guided reading sessions, children can be asked to identify why the writer starts a new paragraph. In stories, paragraphs are often used to:

- Add suspense or change the mood.
- Introduce a new theme.
- Move between time/flashbacks.
- Introduce a new speaker.

Also the way paragraphs are linked can be identified including the way the writer:

- uses connectives
- refers backwards or forwards
- refers to characters (e.g. None of this bothered Kara . . .)
- refers to settings (e.g. use of prepositions: Under that mountain, a dragon lived.)

The connective game

Give children a number of connectives and a context for them to tell a story. This can be done either as a whole class or group. The pupils are shown a picture and range of connectives. They are asked to create a story using the connectives. The connectives do not have to be used in order and others can be used if they prefer.

Picture	Connectives to use	Example text
	One day . . . Fortunately. . . After a while. . . A moment later. . . Meanwhile . . . Unfortunately. . .	One day a dragon landed in the school field. After a while, one brave teacher shuffled outside to investigate. A moment later a police car drove up. Meanwhile, on the other side of town, the dragon slayer left home. Unfortunately he forgot to bring his dragon net that day.
	Initially. . . Subsequently. . . Eventually . . . Afterwards. . . At last. . . Once. . . In the end. . .	Initially no one wanted to take the dog for a walk. Eventually though, the eldest son, who was called Jack, agreed to go. Once he left the house it started to pour with rain. Subsequently the dog got really muddy. Jack and the dog reached home and were greeted like conquering heroes. In the end, Mum made them a cup of delicious hot chocolate.

Pronoun resolution

In the *English grammar, punctuation and spelling test* children are asked to choose the correct pronoun within a sentence. Sentences can be given for pupils to correct, e.g. 'Once upon a time there is three of them'. Alternatively use a text as a model but replace all the nouns with pronouns for the children to improve so that it makes sense e.g. 'Once upon a time there were three of them. In the spring they crossed it to reach it on the other side. But under it he lived. The first to reach it was him. Trip, trap went his little hooves. 'Who's that trip, trapping over it?' he roared'.

Overuse of nouns

Use a text as a model with all pronouns replaced by nouns for children to improve e.g. 'Tom sat down and Tom read the book. Tom couldn't wait to find out what might happen next in the book. The book was a gift from Tom's friend. Tom and his friend both loved to read adventure books'.

With all the above activities it is important that the grammar and punctuation are made explicit so that when children reach Year 6 the terminology is familiar. A whole-school approach to the teaching of grammar and punctuation is needed if children are to succeed at both the *English grammar, punctuation and spelling test* and end of key stage moderation.

7
Apply: Proofreading and editing

'So the writer who breeds more words than he needs, is making a chore for the reader who reads.'

Dr. Seuss

Key concept

Proofreading and editing has been an aspect of writing often missing in recent years. This might partially be blamed on the *Primary Framework* (2006) which defined literacy broadly into three phases:

- reading and immersion in the text type
- speaking and listening and planning
- writing.

The result was that in many schools, children often simply did not write often enough and there was no expectation that work would be developed and improved.

In this chapter you will:
- **learn how to support pupils to proof read and edit their own work**
- **be able to give high quality oral and written feedback**
- **develop guided writing so work is matched precisely to the needs of the pupil**
- **know how to support children to make improvements at word, sentence and text level**

Proofreading and editing within the 2014 curriculum

Proofreading and editing has a much more prominent profile within the 2014 National Curriculum for English. In Years 5 and 6 for example children are expected to evaluate and edit by:

- assessing the effectiveness of their own and others' writing
- proposing changes to vocabulary, grammar and punctuation to enhance effects and clarify meaning

- ensuring the consistent and correct use of tense throughout a piece of writing
- ensuring correct subject and verb agreement when using singular and plural, distinguishing between the language of speech and writing and choosing the appropriate register; proofread for spelling and punctuation errors.

In this chapter, we explore how marking, proofreading and editing help develop pupils' writing, particularly in relation to grammar and punctuation. The Sutton Trust (2011) identified marking and feedback as the most cost effective way to support educational outcomes for disadvantaged pupils.

Teaching ideas

Re-reading writing

This is an essential first step in the editing process and one that teachers often comment as having most impact. At the start of an editing session, children should first take time to re-read their work out loud, to either another child or an adult. This allows for a sense of audience and children will often notice mistakes at this stage, such as missing words or full stops.

Understandably, given the complex nature of writing, many children do not want to proofread or edit their writing. Once completed, boys in particular want to put a piece of work aside and not look at it again. However, this is not what real writers do, a significant amount of time is needed to make changes and craft writing. Dylan Thomas, for example, reportedly once spent a whole day looking at the best place to put one word within a sentence. Using the strategies suggested below, pupils start to realise the importance of drafting and take more pride in their own word. This is also an important skill in relation to the *English grammar, punctuation and spelling test*, where children are often asked to make improvements and correct errors.

Sharing objectives and success criteria

The starting point for any marking and feedback has to be the learning objective. To what extent have pupils achieved what you wanted from them and how can their work be further improved? The objective should lead both the lesson and the feedback and needs to be broken down further into success criteria.

This diagram opposite shows one possible way of doing this. This is intended as a visual representation of a learning journey, rather than a format for planning. Objectives are shown at the top. The progression in grammar grids were then used to support and break these down further. These can then be used to develop success criteria with the children.

Taking the second objective from the diagram for example; describe settings and characters, pupils can be asked what they need to do to achieve this. They might talk in terms of using descriptive language and describing how the character moves and talks. Similes might also be identified. So the success criteria for the children might be:

To describe my setting and character by:

- using description and expanded noun phrases
- using precise vocabulary to create suitable shades in meaning e.g. quite slowly

- describing what characters do and how they do it, using adverbs and adverbial phrases
- using similes and metaphors.

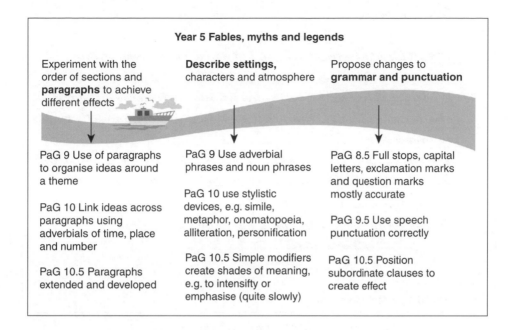

Year 5 Fables, myths and legends

Experiment with the order of sections and **paragraphs** to achieve different effects

Describe settings, characters and atmosphere

Propose changes to **grammar and punctuation**

PaG 9 Use of paragraphs to organise ideas around a theme

PaG 10 Link ideas across paragraphs using adverbials of time, place and number

PaG 10.5 Paragraphs extended and developed

PaG 9 Use adverbial phrases and noun phrases

PaG 10 use stylistic devices, e.g. simile, metaphor, onomatopoeia, alliteration, personification

PaG 10.5 Simple modifiers create shades of meaning, e.g. to intensifty or emphasise (quite slowly)

PaG 8.5 Full stops, capital letters, exclamation marks and question marks mostly accurate

PaG 9.5 Use speech punctuation correctly

PaG 10.5 Position subordinate clauses to create effect

The intention isn't necessarily to cover all this in one lesson. It depends on where the children are and prior learning. However, it is intended that the more able get further as many of these skills are known. When I model a lesson teachers are often surprised by how I develop success criteria with the children, but this is essential if they are to be both meaningful and owned by pupils. These are then used throughout the lesson and to edit their work against. While feedback is first and foremost against the objective other elements should not be ignored. For example, a child might use a skill taught earlier, such as using a range of connectives. Such moments should be celebrated and in terms of assessment, provide much clearer evidence than a skill that is applied immediately after teaching.

Oral and written feedback

In the example below, the teacher highlights where the child has met the learning intention and an area for improvement. There are a number of possible ways to show this. Positive aspects might be identified using double ticks, or sentences might be highlighted. Popular phrases in schools include golden lines (where an orange pen is used) or tickled pink (using a pink pen). The important point is, that if the teacher **does not** identify what is good about a piece of work an important learning opportunity is missed, as well as having a negative impact on motivation.

In a similar way an area for improvement needs to be identified. A popular phrase here is green for growth, which gives the impression of a positive activity, rather than correction.

27th June 1941

Dear Imogen,

It's still quite busy at school, but some people are staying at home because there are quite a lot of bombs going off still. When I get home, mum is always in our Anderson shelter – she's really scared. Dad's factory has shut down so he's trying to find a new job.

It's really hard for everyone. We've put black-out curtains up. Anyway, who ~~are~~ were you put with? ~~The~~ Is she/he nice? Are you having a good time? Do you miss me? I miss you! Please write back! How long did your journey take?

        Best wishes,

          x x x x

How did you feel about this?

APP writing standards file: Kylie, Department for Education

The example above shows one possible approach to marking and feedback. The teacher has highlighted the first three sentences as good examples of writing, where the child has managed to include the features asked for within the success criteria. In the first two sentences, Kylie has used complex sentences and in the third talks about her feelings.

'Green for growth' has then been used to identify an area to improve. The child is then encouraged to make the amendment through a reminder prompt. It is important that the child actually makes the improvement, rather than just being asked to use a skill in the future. A comment such as 'Remember to use adverbial phrases', does not have the same impact. The child might not get the opportunity at some future date so the skill needs to be applied to the piece of writing and this is the first step in pupils editing their work.

The teacher needs to model the process so children understand how to make improvements. A visualiser, photograph or enlarged copy can be used to identify success and make improvements. Presentation is important, by both the teacher and the child when making amendments. Once the process is understood the children can start identifying where they have met the learning intention themselves and areas to improve on. This can also be done with a response partner, though it is important that the pupil whose work it is amends their own writing. Oral feedback is even more powerful and this can be achieved during guided writing sessions.

Guided writing

Guided writing is a period of time that slots in between shared writing and the plenary, where the teacher sits with a group of children to further support them towards independence, while the rest of the class work independently. Roger Beard, emphasises, 'the potential of guided writing for improving syntactical structure and grammatical awareness within particular genres.' (p1,Beard, 2001).

The DfEE in *Grammar for Writing* (2000), suggests three purposes for guided writing:

- To support children in planning and drafting their own writing. Work is carefully scaffolded so that pupils can concentrate on one particular aspect of their work.
- To help revise and edit work in progress.
- To provide differentiated support for particular groups. This may take the form of a mini-lesson based on work done in shared writing.

An important aspect of guided writing is that it allows the teacher to intervene at the point of writing. As children write, the teacher can see what is happening and make suggestions. Where a child uses overly extended sentences, they can be asked to read their writing aloud so that they hear where the pauses should go. Children can be asked to orally rehearse sentences with a partner or write on a whiteboard, though there needs to be some writing in the books as well. Groupings should be flexible, with children who struggle with a concept being brought together. The adult is not chained to the group, there needs to be a degree of independence, so the teacher can take moments to check how the rest of the class is getting on.

Guided writing can slow the pace but allows for precision teaching and faster progress. Children often write enthusiastically but get carried away and need to slow down. The analogy is like riding a horse, the rider needs to be in charge, not the horse. If children do not take care and pride in their work, sentence structure and punctuation will suffer. Also the teacher should not be crouched behind pupils, working with one child while the rest wait to know what happens next. One useful technique is that the children are sat as shown here:

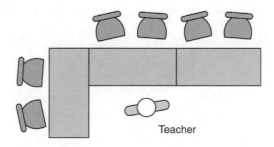

Teacher

The tables are arranged at right angles so that all the children are facing the teacher and all the children's work can be clearly seen. Learning support assistants (LSAs) can be used in a similar way to support children's writing. However the recommendations of the report *Deployment and Impact of Support Staff in Schools* (2009), should be taken into account. If the following recommendations are in place the impact will be greater:

- Deployment – LSAs should not always be working with the least able. This is the most vulnerable group within the classroom and as such need the support of the most qualified adult.
- LSAs need to be trained and their subject knowledge developed if they are to support pupils effectively.
- Communication between the teacher and the LSA is crucial and time needs to be taken to ensure this happens.

Making improvements

Word level

Making improvements at word level is relatively straightforward. The sentence can be highlighted and children prompted to add the part of speech identified, such as adding an adjective or improving the verb. The skill can be reinforced through asking the child to suggest different alternatives, e.g. in the sentence identified add three powerful verbs that could be used to replace the word 'went'.

The cat **went** down the path. (replacement verbs: hurried, slunk, scampered)

Once children understand the basic parts of speech they then can be asked to use phrases, e.g. expand the noun phrase and add an adverbial clause:

The cat slunk down the path.

The black and white tabby with the torn ear slunk down the path in the middle of the night.

Making such improvements from within the children's own writing mirrors the games and activities suggested earlier and are similar to the tasks in the *English grammar, punctuation and spelling test*.

Sentence level

When making improvements at sentence level, discussion is essential and the process needs to be clearly modelled. Children need to get the basics right first, sentence structure can be seen as a progression. If they are not writing in sentences, introducing complex sentences may create further confusion. Discussing what a sentence is can be helpful and useful if displayed. These suggestions were made by pupils. Comments such as 'they have a capital letter and full stop' do not help initially, the problem is identifying where these go. That they 'make sense in their own right' helps when looking at one phrase

but is less useful when looking at a whole text. The fact a full stop helps identify 'where to take a breath' is useful and proofreading can be an ideal opportunity to discuss punctuation. Children's own definitions can also be very useful; one child with an interest in motorbikes described a sentence as, 'Where I change from one thought to another, like when I stop talking about the throttle and move onto the brakes.' An understanding of what a noun and a verb is can also be useful.

Children should identify where the punctuation or grammatical features go for themselves. There is little learning in circling where the full stops should be for them. Marking and feedback should always involve more work for the child than for the adult. It is better therefore just to make a comment, such as: Two full stops are missing, can you identify where?

Once the children can identify clauses they are ready to join sentences using compound conjunctions.

Complex sentences and adverbial phrases

Children can be asked to add a subordinate clause or adverbial phrase to a sentence. For example the child might have written: *'The boy sprinted for the finish line.'*

The teacher might prompt, asking for a subordinate clause to add more information. You might want to further scaffold the learning through giving a range of possible connectives to get them started such as while, although, however: *e.g. While the crowd cheered loudly, the boy sprinted for the finish line.*

Adverbial phrases can be added in a similar way, for example the child might add a phrase to describe where, when or how the boy sprinted: *e.g. At the last minute, the boy sprinted for the finish line.*

Children can also be asked to:

- Add a different sentence type – e.g. a question or command.
- Add a short sentence for impact.
- Punctuate a passage to avoid overly extended sentences, or insert the identified punctuation within a paragraph e.g. insert the ! ? :, .
- Add figurative language such as a simile or idiom (e.g. too many cooks spoil the broth).

Editing for text cohesion

When editing, children might be asked to add phrases to make it more exciting for the reader or to make it more persuasive, etc. Children can also be asked to attend to other aspects of text cohesion, for example checking:

- Events are in a logical order.
- Information has not been left out.
- Ideas are elaborated upon.
- Paragraph breaks are put in.
- It is clear to whom the pronoun refers.

- A pronoun is used to avoid repeating a noun.
- Verb tenses are consistent.
- Paragraphs start or end with a connective that helps link the content.
- Within paragraphs ideas are linked using a range of connectives.

Once a piece of work has been completed it is important that it is celebrated. A portfolio approach can work well, with children choosing favourite pieces of work to publish. These can be displayed or put into class anthologies. This helps the child see themselves as a real writer and gives a purpose to the experience. Children can also publish work easily online to share with the wider community.

The ability of pupils to make their own improvements is an essential part of becoming a successful writer and one that children need to pay attention to. The fact that it is such a key feature of the 2014 National Curriculum for English is welcomed. Also making amendments to their own work equips pupils to be able to do the same with the questions in the *English grammar, punctuation and spelling test*.

8
The balance of writing and case studies

You will never find time for anything. If you want time you must make it.

Charles Buxton

Key concept

In this chapter, I explore the balance of writing and how best to motivate children to develop as writers, using grammar and punctuation effectively. The aim is for the punctuation and grammar to become embedded in their writing. While we want children to succeed in the *English grammar, punctuation and spelling test* they must also be able to write coherently with real purposes and audiences in mind. At the end of each key stage children's writing is moderated using a range of evidence and it is within this context that this chapter focuses. Examples of children's work are used to help illustrate how best to develop grammar in context.

In this chapter you will:

- **know how grammar and punctuation fits within the full range of skills needed to write**
- **learn how to support the development of pupil's grammar through the content of their writing, audience and purpose**
- **be able to develop basic skills and high expectations**
- **develop assessment to support teaching and learning**
- **be able to support the more able**

Case studies

Two primary schools have been used as case studies and, for the purpose of anonymity, the names of the schools and children have been changed.

- Phoenix Primary – set in a ward of high relative disadvantage, 30% of pupils have free school meals. Traditional school improvement and recovery processes had been exhausted and therefore a new headteacher and management team were appointed. Due to strong leadership, the school has now been judged to be outstanding. The project focused on a group of lower attaining pupils and the impact of a number of teaching techniques on their punctuation and grammar.

- Freeway Primary – a smaller school where most pupils are White British and speak English as their first language. The proportion of disabled pupils and those with special educational needs is above average.

The importance of good leadership to drive forward change cannot be underestimated. In both schools the ethos was such that teaching and learning were given the highest priority. Once an issue was identified, time was taken to address it, and if this meant changing the timetables so be it!

However, should one aspect take greater priority and what about motivation and writing? Writing is a complex process where children have to concentrate on a number of aspects, as shown in the diagram below:

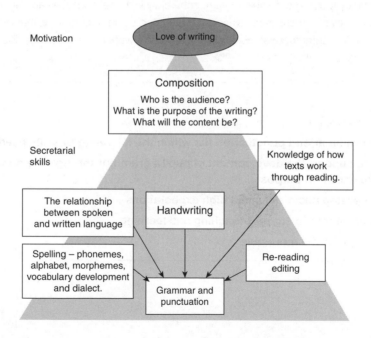

The analogy is like driving a car, when you first start to drive you have to think: signal, mirror, handbrake, clutch and manoeuvre. Yet over time this becomes automatic. It is little wonder, given the complexity of the writing process that children find it difficult to apply all the skills taught at once. Where pupils concentrate on story structure, the grammar goes and when they focus on sentence structure the reverse is true. There is the added complication of the spiral curriculum; learning is rarely linear, so that a skill learnt may deteriorate when added complexities are introduced. So how can we get children to embed the skills taught, so that they are applied automatically in writing?

Teaching ideas

High expectations and the basics

In both schools, careful timetabling and the teaching of basic skills was the starting point to driving up standards. At Phoenix Primary pupils took little pride in their work, resulting in scribbling on books and poor quality writing. Having high expectations in terms of presentation, including grammar and punctuation, was the starting point. Pupils took the time to see pieces of writing through to publishing and examples were displayed around the school. In all the examples that follow, the first thing that stands out is the improvement in handwriting.

The craft of writing through the act of writing

Plenty of time needs to be given to drafting writing in the first place. This is borne out in the 2012 Ofsted report, *Moving English Forward*, 'A constant criticism from inspectors was that pupils rarely had extended periods to read, write or discuss issues in class. Indeed, inspectors observed lessons where pupils were asked to self- or peer-assess work before they had been able to complete more than a sentence or two.' (p14).

However if children are to write at length they need to be motivated. The research shows that children are more motivated by real writing, with a purpose and audience in mind, rather than decontextualised activities.

At Freeway Primary, the key issues identified included: pupils were too passive; more opportunities to write at length were needed; and there was insufficient challenge, particularly for the more able. Therefore a questionnaire was used to identify more able pupil's views about writing:

Questioning more able children about writing

- Do you enjoy writing?
- What inspires you to write?
- What do you enjoy writing about?
- How would you recommend writing to somebody else?

The main finding was that the pupils enjoyed writing but would like to write more, especially stories. One child wrote, 'I'd like to write more stories and poems because at the moment we do a lot of comprehension.'

Perhaps it is to be expected that more able pupils enjoy writing, but the findings were also borne out with less able pupils at Phoenix Primary. Pupils were taught a series of lesson and asked to rate them on a scale from 1 to 10.

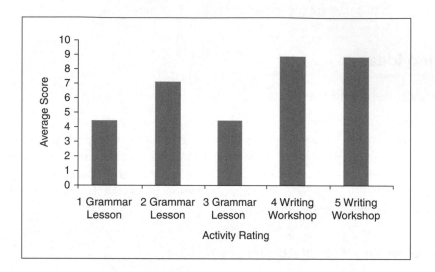

The first three lessons were taught using more traditional grammar teaching methods. In Lesson 1, for example, children were given a text and asked to identify the nouns; whiteboards and an interactive style of teaching were used. In Lessons 4 and 5 a writing workshop model was used. A quality text was enjoyed for its own sake first, and then using modelled writing, children wrote a story in a similar style. Discussion about grammar and punctuation arose naturally from the writing.

The writing workshop sessions were most popular. The children commented on how much they had enjoyed the story. One boy commented 'I enjoyed writing and learnt how to use connectives.' Out of the more formal grammar sessions, Lesson 2 was rated more highly because the work had related more closely to the topic children were studying.

These findings were further confirmed through the classroom assistant's observations. In the writing workshop sessions, all the focus children were concentrating and asked more questions or made responses – a total of 11 in Lesson 4; whereas in Lesson 1, only three questions were asked by the focus group. Children preferred a writing workshop approach, where they enjoyed a quality text for its own sake and grammar arose naturally from the text and from their writing.

Content, audience and purpose

At Phoenix Primary it was found the content of the writing had the greatest impact and this was closely related to audience and purpose. If children didn't have enough happening, they resorted to dialogue to try and pad their work out, which was often poorly punctuated. The example below helps illustrate the point.

> The Tramp.
> hid and seek said the dog and Jessie,
> Hollie and Pearl, then Pearl said I will
> aske my mum if the dog Jessie and
> Hollie can sleep round my house and we
> can have a midnight snack and in the
> morning my mum can take you lot to
> school and then we can play in the park
> and play it this time.

Speakerly writing

It is often the basics children struggle with – the example above is typical of 'speakerly writing.' This is where the child writes as they speak, without consideration for the reader. The author of the piece, Hiyat, is still working with a PaG age of 6, despite being in Year 5. It is a style of writing that teachers most frequently ask for advice on. While another person is able to read the writing, Hiyat needs to use full stops and capital letters. It was found that with the group of less able pupils quick improvement could be made. The following piece of work is by Hiyat later in the year.

> The amazing Wan Hu.
>
> One day Wan Hu came across the door. He glansed around so he could not get coute. So he crept to the door and he opened it and ran to his friends house. While he was walking to his friends house he saw an alleyway and he thought it was quicker. But when he was at the end of the alleyway he saw his friend house was five doors away and he ran there.

A writing workshop approach was used in which the story structure of a number of texts were analysed. Children planned their stories with a clear ending in mind. This time the punctuation was much better, with full stops correctly placed on average eight out of ten times. Though there is still plenty of room for improvement the work shows the application of skills of a child with a PaG age of 8. Methods that took the writing forward are described below.

Audience and purpose

Children need to write with a clear sense of audience and purpose. Hiyat didn't consider the reader when writing. Asking Hiyat to read her writing aloud to either the teacher or another child had a significant impact.

The content of the writing

If children don't have enough happening within their writing, or are unsure where the writing is heading, they often resort to dialogue to try and pad their work out, which is often poorly punctuated. Hiyat was used to writing about her visit to the shops or talking to her friends. As soon as an event happened, such as a volcano erupting, the punctuation improved. Planning writing in advance greatly helped her punctuation.

Reading habits

The initial writing reflected Hiyat's poor reading habits. Many poor writers are reluctant to read and do not understand how texts and stories work. Therefore it is crucial that these children are encouraged to read and see good examples of quality texts. If the child is not reading at home, it is essential they do so at school.

Assessment for Learning

In the first example of Hiyat's writing, a total of 17 'ands' were used over ten sentences; no capital letters or full stops were used. Hiyat was given a clear target, to try and reduce the number of 'ands' and to use more full stops.

Bicycle
It is a ~~gtis~~ girls ~~olt~~ ~~grips~~
bick and the black grips.
and The bicycle his got
silver spokes. Its got and
purple handle bars. With
black sking. Seat. and it is
Purple with a black happie
face base. And White head
lithe. And on the back it
got a red head

Example A

Fantasy Kingdom
Everybody loves a funfair. Well come
on down to fantasy kingdom. You
can scream on the flying fox. It goes
up, down and all around, at break-
neck speed.

Also you can go on the cable car to
the scenic ride to ice mountain. On
the top of the ice mountain is Ice
palace you can get yummy waffles
and real snow all year round.

Example B

Bringing children's attention to the text level features of non-fiction texts can have a similar impact. In example A the child wrote with no audience or purpose in mind. The work is poorly punctuated and 'and' is repeated on a number of occasions.

Example B is from the same child a term later. He began by writing a radio advert for a new funfair, using drama to stimulate writing. The purpose of the writing was to persuade and sentence punctuation is significantly improved. It was also found that writing in paragraphs also significantly impacts on grammar and punctuation. Children should be encouraged to look at the features of paragraphs in relation to both non-fiction and fiction in a similar way to what was discussed in the previous chapter. Through editing and publishing their own work, children developed their work further and paid more attention to grammar and punctuation.

Grammar and the more able

At Freeway Primary, pupils were given more freedom, choice and opportunities to write more frequently. They identified their own samples of writing to work on, using a portfolio approach and these were used to edit and work up to publication. Alongside this, teachers introduced two short grammar sessions a week to use the grammar games and activities suggested.

In the autumn term, children's writing was monitored from Year 3 to Year 6, and again at the end of the spring term. Teachers were surprised by the initial findings, especially by the fact that so few able pupils were using figurative language.

Grammatical features identified

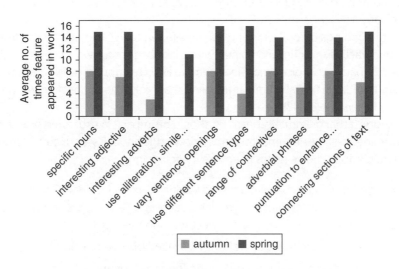

Over the period between the autumn term and the spring term all children's writing greatly improved across the areas identified and good progress was made. The sample below shows how the writing flows in a natural way with a clear sense of audience and purpose using a range of sentence lengths. The grammar isn't forced, as can be the case when the emphasis is solely on grammar.

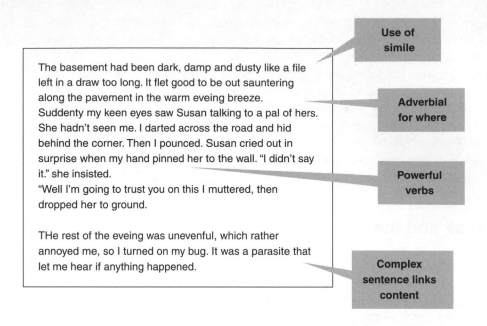

The basement had been dark, damp and dusty like a file left in a draw too long. It flet good to be out sauntering along the pavement in the warm eveing breeze.

Suddenty my keen eyes saw Susan talking to a pal of hers. She hadn't seen me. I darted across the road and hid behind the corner. Then I pounced. Susan cried out in surprise when my hand pinned her to the wall. "I didn't say it." she insisted.

"Well I'm going to trust you on this I muttered, then dropped her to ground.

THe rest of the eveing was unevenful, which rather annoyed me, so I turned on my bug. It was a parasite that let me hear if anything happened.

Use of simile

Adverbial for where

Powerful verbs

Complex sentence links content

Conclusion

Research shows, that the use of decontextualised activities, that involve identifying and correcting parts of speech, have little direct impact on pupil's writing. The success of teaching in context within pupil's own writing, concentrating on modelled writing; short practise activities; and editing and proofreading, is evident, particularly from the samples of work.

This confirms the findings of Tomlinson and others referred to in Chapter 2. 'The safest conclusion to be drawn . . . is that practice in writing, combined with a language focus which routinely draws attention to language features, patterns, choices and effects is more likely to improve pupils' grammatical range and competence than traditional formal grammar teaching that makes no connection with pupils language use.' (*The Grammar Papers*, 1998, p48).

This is not to suggest that grammatical learning should be implicit. A structured programme is needed to ensure full coverage of all the grammatical terms, knowledge and skills required. In summary, any good grammar and punctuation scheme needs to ensure the following:

- Teaching starts from looking at the whole text to identify its main features; audience and purpose being of prime concern. Text features are identified, success criteria shared and writing modelled. Grammar is explicitly taught in context and correct terminology used.

- Pupils plan their writing but in doing so are given considerable freedom and choice.

- A significant amount of time is given to children drafting their writing, while the teacher works with a group guiding the writing.

- During this process time is taken to practise skills taught through short games and activities.

- Work is then proofread and edited, either individually or with a partner and time is taken to make amendments and respond to marking and feedback.
- Finally some pieces of writing can be chosen to further refine and publish.

The overall aim of this book is to drive up standards in relation to writing, punctuation and grammar and the approach suggested, based on research and best practice should have a direct impact. Experience shows that teaching to a test, through a narrow curriculum does not achieve the best results. The broadening of the curriculum and changes to assessment offers schools a real opportunity to make a difference, so children can succeed as writers. Knowledge and skills gained through this approach will also mean that children achieve well at the end of key stage tests and within the *English grammar, punctuation and spelling test*.

Appendix 1 – Progression in grammar grids

Progression in Grammar – with matched sub levels (fine grades)

	Grammar and sentence structure	Punctuation	Terminology for pupils
PaG age 5.5 (*Level 1c / 1b APS 9*)	• Knows words combine to make sentences • Separation of words with spaces • Uses simple words, phrases or captions	• Some awareness of use of full stops and capital letters • Read writing back, with appropriate pauses	word letter sentence capital letter full stop punctuation
PaG age 6 (*Level 1a APS 11*)	• Use adjectives occasionally (e.g. big, red) • Write some grammatically accurate clauses (e.g. he went to the shop, he ran to the park) • Beginning to use and to join sentences • Some events/ideas in appropriate order e.g. actions listed in time/sequence/items numbered • Simple connections between ideas, events, e.g. repeated nouns, pronouns	• Capital letters for names and for the personal pronoun I • Sometimes punctuate a sentence with both a full stop and capital letter • Introduction to the use of question marks and exclamation marks	singular plural question mark exclamation mark
PaG age 6.5 (end of Y1) (*Level 2c APS 13*)	• Can identify verbs in the present or past tense • Use precise nouns e.g. spaniel rather than dog • Accurate use of simple sentences that contain a noun, a verb and sometimes an adjective e.g. The big dog barked • Beginning to vary sentence openings e.g. not always starting with name or pronoun • Use simple conjunctions (e.g. and, but) • The consistent use of present tense versus past tense	• Primarily simple and compound sentences working towards grammatical accuracy • Sentences usually demarcated by capital letters and full stops. Some use of question and exclamation marks and commas in a list	noun past tense present tense

	Grammar and sentence structure	Punctuation	Terminology for pupils
PaG age 7 (Level 2b APS 15)	• Can identify nouns, verbs and adjectives • Adjectives used to add details and chosen thoughtfully • Verb choice is descriptive / appropriate • Sentences with different forms: statement, question, exclamation, command • Includes some simple variation (Today was exciting. . . Yesterday we went . . .) • Clauses joined by and, but, so, or • Ideas in sections grouped by content, some linking by simple pronouns	• Uses commas to separate items in a list • Sentence structure mostly grammatically correct	verb adjective comma statement question exclamation command
PaG age 7.5 (end of Y2) (Level 2a APS 17 Consolidation of level 2)	• Some detail included through adventurous word choice appropriate to task (a big, hairy caterpillar . . . Mr Jones looked cross . . .) • Expanded noun phrases for description and specification (e.g. the blue butterfly, the man in the moon) • Adverbs tell the reader when, where and how things happen • Use of the progressive form of verbs to mark actions in progress (e.g. she is drumming, he was shouting) • Use appropriate connectives to structure ideas logically, including for time (after, first) • Uses when, if, that, or because for subordination • Some attempt to sequence ideas or events, e.g. by use of time related words; numbered points; headings, line breaks; use of pictures • Use of the continuous form of verbs in the present and past tense to mark actions in progress (e.g. she is drumming, he was shouting)	• Apostrophes to mark contracted forms in spelling • Sentence demarcation with capital letters and full stops usually accurate • Some accurate use of question marks and exclamation marks, and commas in lists	adverb apostrophe connective

Progression in Grammar – with matched sub levels (fine grades)

	Grammar and sentence structure	Punctuation	Terminology for pupils
PaG age 8 *(Level 3c APS 19)*	• Can identify nouns, verbs, adjectives and prepositions • Some attempt to elaborate on basic information • Expressing time and cause through: conjunctions (e.g. when, before, after); adverbs (e.g. then, next, so); and prepositions (e.g. before, after, during) • Begin to use ways other than the subject to start sentences e.g. Today, I ate a cake • Can substitute nouns with simple pronouns and use pronouns to avoid repetition e.g. it, he, they, she). • Show a general understanding of simple past and present tense and usually have correct subject and verb agreement (was/ were) • Consistency with the use of the first and third person • Begin to use paragraphs to group related material	• Beginning to use speech marks to punctuate direct speech • Accurately use commas in lists	word family conjunction adverb preposition direct speech inverted commas (or 'speech marks') clause paragraphs
PaG age 8.5 (end of Y3) *(Level 3b APS 21)*	• Can identify and use expanded noun phrases to add interest and detail • Use a variety of sentence openings to avoid repetition (e.g. then, next). • Use a variety of conjunctions to clarify relationship between ideas (e.g. but, so, when, because, while) • Use fronted adverbials • Within paragraphs/sections, some links between sentences e.g. use of pronouns or adverbials • Appropriate choice of pronoun or noun within a sentence to avoid ambiguity and repetition • Tense choice generally appropriate to task including some use of modals (can, will)	• Apostrophes to mark singular and plural possession (e.g. the girl's name, the boys' boots) • Full stops, capital letters, exclamation marks and question marks mostly accurate • Commas used in lists • Use speech marks to punctuate direct speech • Use of commas after fronted adverbials (e.g. Later that day, I heard the bad news.)	pronoun possessive pronoun adverbial phrase noun phrase

Progression in Grammar – with matched sub Levels (fine grades)

Age	Grammar and sentence structure	Punctuation	Terminology
PaG age 9 *(Level 3a APS 23)*	• Some detail/description of events or ideas expanded through vocabulary (simple adverbs, adjectives) or explanation. Some vocabulary selected for effect or appropriateness to task • Use adverbial phrases and noun phrases to give clarity to the account • May include complex sentences. Use of when, because, or, if) • Extend the range of sentences with more than one clause by using a wider range of connectives e.g. when, if, because, although • Some sentence variation created, e.g. direct speech; simple adverbials (we played after tea. . . it was scary in the tunnel) • Features of writing generally appropriate to the selected task, e.g. use of dialogue in a story; first person for a letter; imperative in instructions • Simple adverbials/pronouns may link sentences, sections or paragraphs (when we got there, after that) • Use of paragraphs to organise ideas around a theme	• Use and experiment with a range of punctuation, although not always accurately e.g. brackets, semi-colon, colon and dash	adverbial phrase dash subordinate clause bracket cohesion

PaG age 9.5 (end of Y4) *(Consolidation of Level 2 and 3)*	• Familiar with a range of word classes including adverbs and prepositions • Noun phrases expanded by the addition of modifying adjectives, nouns and preposition phrases (e.g. *the teacher* expanded to: *the strict maths teacher with curly hair*) • Some variety in subordinating conjuctions: because, if, which (because the rain can damage their skin. . .which was strange. . .If she could . . .) • Sentences are grammatically sound, e.g. correct subject/verb agreement; security of tense and person; correct use of subordination. • Recognise and write different types of sentences when prompted e.g. imperatives in commands • Identify and use subordinate clauses to form straightforward complex sentences • Use some variety in length, subject or structure of sentences • Appropriate choice of pronoun or noun within and across sentences to aid cohesion and avoid repetition • Paragraphs/sections help to organise content, e.g. main idea usually supported or elaborated by following sentences • Understand some features of the grammar of standard English	• Use the apostrophe for omission accurately • Sometimes use commas to separate phrases or clauses, although not always accurately. • Use speech punctuation (inverted commas) correctly with a new line for each speaker	determiner subordinate clause complex sentence adverbial relative clause relative pronoun, ambiguity tense choice

Progression in Grammar – with matched sub levels (fine grades)

Age	Grammar and sentence structure	Punctuation	Terminology
PaG age 10 (Level 4c APS 25)	• Show understanding of a variety of verb forms, e.g. past, present, continuous • Choices of vocabulary generally accurate when selecting synonyms and antonyms • Indicating degrees of possibility using adverbs (e.g. perhaps, surely) or modal verbs (e.g. might, should, will, must) • Use adverbials and expanded noun phrases to engage as well as inform • Use stylistic devices, e.g. simile, metaphor, onomatopoeia, alliteration, personification • Experiment with complex sentences to clarify relationship in time and place • Use a range of openings, e.g. adverbials (some time later, as we ran . . .), subject reference (they, the boys, our gang . . .), and speech. • Use commas to mark clauses or phrases • Use inverted commas to denote speech, and apostrophes for omission • Use a wider range of sentence connectives to develop meaning e.g, if, when, rather than, although, however • Features of text type/genre are appropriate to the task, e.g. choice of tense / verb form; layout; formality. Ideas may be adapted, e.g. inclusion of contextual information on a fictitious character or the use of quotes within a report • Link ideas across paragraphs using adverbials of time (e.g. later), place (e.g. nearby) and number (e.g. secondly)	• Most sentences correctly demarcated, e.g. apostrophes mark contractions. If used, inverted commas demarcate the beginning and end of direct speech, correctly on most occasions • Brackets, dashes or commas to indicate parenthesis (a word or phrase added as an explanation or afterthought) • Use of commas to clarify meaning or avoid ambiguity	modal verb subordinate clause adverbial expanded noun phrases

- Ideas and events developed through some deliberate selection of phrases and vocabulary, e.g. technical terminology; vivid language; word choice for effect or emphasis
- Simple modifiers may create shades of meaning, e.g. to intensify or emphasise (very large, quite slowly)
- Some use of stylistic features support purpose, e.g. formal / informal vocabulary; appropriate use of similes
- Use relative clauses beginning with who, which, where, why, or whose
- Position subordinate clauses to create effect
- Use of the passive voice to affect the presentation of information in a sentence (e.g. I broke the window in the greenhouse versus The window in the greenhouse was broken)
- Variety in sentence length, structure and subject to help expand ideas, convey key issues/facts or provide emphasis, detail and description
- Paragraphs or sections may be extended and developed, usually around a topic, main point, event, or idea, e.g. with explanation, contrast, additional detail
- Devices to build cohesion within a paragraph (e.g. then, after that, this, firstly)
- Tense choice appropriate with verb forms varied and generally accurate, including the use of modals to express prediction, possibility, permission, e.g. should, might, could

- Use apostrophe for both omission and singular possession
- Use commas to separate phrases or clauses accurately
- Experiment with a wider range of punctuation, e.g. brackets, dashes, colon, semi-colon
- Use speech marks (inverted commas) with confidence in sentences (e.g. for reported speech and internal character dialogue)

simile
metaphor
onomatopoeia
alliteration
personification
active and passive voice
colon
semi-colon
bullet points

Progression in Grammar – with matched sub levels (fine grades)

Level	Grammar and sentence structure	Punctuation
PaG age 11 (Level 4a APS 29)	<ul><li>A secure understanding of most word classes listed in the programme of study</li><li>Use expanded noun phrases to convey complicated information concisely (e.g. the boy that jumped over the fence is over there, or the fact that it was raining meant the end of sports day)</li><li>Beginning to use more complex verb forms, including modals</li><li>Children's understanding of a variety of sentence structures is mostly secure, including fronted adverbials and embedded relative clauses</li><li>Use different sentence types, e.g. questions, direct / reported speech, commands used appropriately</li><li>Use a variety of sentence lengths, structures and subjects to provide clarity and emphasis (e.g. through the use of active/passive voice)</li><li>Use grammatically complex sentences (i.e. is able to position and punctuate subordinate clauses)</li><li>Use a more formal tone with confidence when appropriate</li><li>Layout devices, such as headings, sub-headings, columns, bullets, or tables, to structure text</li><li>Features of selected form are clearly established, e.g. appropriate selection and variation of tense; choice of person; level of formality; adaptation of content for genre and audience.</li><li>Overall organisation of text is supported by paragraphs or sections which enable coherent development and control of content across the text</li></ul>	Use of the semi-colon, colon and dash to indicate a stronger subdivision of a sentence than a comma Punctuation of bullet points to list information **Terminology for pupils** subject and object complex sentence noun phrase formal tone adverbial semi-colon colon dash verb forms colloquial and standard English cohesion

PaG age 11.5 (end of Y6) (Level 5c APS 31)

- Precise word choice create impact and augment meaning
- The difference between informal and formal speech (e.g. find out – discover; ask for – request; go in – enter)
- Additional words and phrases contribute to shades of meaning e.g. Joe was_____ when his cat went missing. [sad, depressed, heartbroken])
- Ensure writing uses an appropriate range of figurative language to enhance the narrative
- Variety in sentence length, structure and subject to help expand ideas, convey key issues/facts or provide emphasis, detail and description
- A range of verb forms develops meaning and maintains appropriate tense choice (it will probably leave of its own accord. . . We could catch a later train, but will we arrive on time?)
- Show some contrast between colloquial or standard English
- Relationships between paragraphs or sections give structure to the whole text, e.g. links make structure between topics clear; connections between opening and ending
- Use of the passive to affect the presentation of information in a sentence (e.g. I broke the window in the greenhouse versus The window in the greenhouse was broken [by me])
- Content is balanced and controlled with some effective selection and ordering of text to engage the reader, e.g. placement of significant idea/event for emphasis; reflective comment; opinion; dialogue

- How hyphens can be used to avoid ambiguity (e.g. man eating shark versus man-eating shark)
- Range of punctuation used, almost always correctly, e.g. brackets, dashes, colons
- Correctly demarcate sentences with intra-sentence punctuation e.g. dashes, parenthesis (brackets)
- Use a range of punctuation appropriately to add humour or enhance description

Terminology for pupils

figurative language
subjunctive
intra-sentence punctuation
hyphen

Progression in Grammar – with matched sub levels (fine grades)

Level	Grammar and sentence structure	Punctuation
PaG age 12 (Level 5b APS 33)	• Modifiers contribute to shades of meaning, e.g. adverbs (extremely) • Some features of sentence structure used to build up detail or convey shades of meaning e.g. variation in word order, expansions in verb phrases • Varied stylistic features support both purpose and effect, e.g. metaphors, puns, emotive phrases • A range of subordinate connectives (while, until, despite) with possible use of several subordinate clauses to aid economy of expression (Because of their courageous efforts, all of the passengers were saved, which was nothing short of a miracle. . . 'While under my roof, you will obey my rules, which are clearly displayed') • A range of verb forms develops meaning, and appropriate tense choice is maintained (It will probably leave of its own accord. . . We could catch a later train, but will we arrive on time?) • Use a more formal tone with confidence when appropriate and show some contrast between colloquial or standard English • Shaping of paragraphs evident to highlight or prioritise information, provide chronological links, build tension or interject comment or reflection • A range of cohesive devices used to develop or elaborate ideas both within and between paragraphs, e.g. pronouns; adverbials; connectives; subject specific vocabulary; phrases or chains of reference (However, it should be stated. . . Biological changes. . . Despite their heroic efforts . . .)	Use a wide range of well controlled punctuation for effect, meaning and pace Use commas within sentences to avoid Show evidence of effective use of colons or dashes to structure longer sentences **Terminology for pupils** subordinate clauses economy of expression

PaG age 12.5 (end of Y7)
(Level 5a APS 35)

- Have a secure understanding of a range of word classes, including different types of nouns and pronouns
- Draw on new vocabulary and grammatical constructions from their reading and listening, and use these consciously in their writing and speech to achieve particular effects
- Additional words and phrases are used for precision and impact (e.g. exceptional result, insignificant amount)
- Ideas are developed through controlled use of elaboration and imaginative detail. Vocabulary is varied and often ambitious
- Analyse the effectiveness and impact of the grammatical features of the texts they read
- Understand how to recognise and use a range of grammatical structures, including complex noun and prepositional phrases
- Children understand and can use embedded subordinate clauses and their control and placement of phrases and clauses within complex sentences is mostly secure
- Ideas and events developed through elaboration, nominalisation, and imaginative detail, e.g. expansion of key events/detailed characterisation
- Secure in their ability to use standard English when appropriate, including subject/verb agreement when experimenting with more sophisticated syntax
- A range of cohesive devices contribute to the effect of the text on the reader and the placing of emphasis for impact (e.g. precise adverbials as sentence starters, a range of appropriate connectives, subject specific vocabulary, select use of pronoun referencing, complex noun phrases, prepositional phrases)

Children can use a full range of punctuation, including colons and semi-colons, correctly and are able to apply these to more sophisticated grammatical structures

Terminology for pupils

figurative language
subordinate connectives
elaboration
viewpoint

Progression in Grammar

Level	Grammar and sentence structure	Punctuation
PaG age 13 (Level 6c APS 37)	• Emphasis created through word order, accurate adaptation of verb phrases, and use of passive (the centre has been visited often) • Demonstrate a wide range of vocabulary from which they make precise choices • Knowing and understanding the differences between spoken and written language, including differences associated with formal and informal registers, and between standard English and other varieties of English • Discuss reading, writing and spoken language with precise and confident use of linguistic and literary terminology • Use a range of verb forms, including complex modals, impersonal constructions and passives for formality • A range of sentence features are used to give clarity or emphasis of meaning (fronted adverbials: As a consequence of. . . Glancing backwards. . . Some weeks later. . . /complex noun phrases: The mysterious young girl in the portrait. . . / prepositional phrases: From behind the bike shed. . . In the event of . . .) • Link ideas across paragraphs using a wider range of cohesive devices: semantic cohesion e.g. repetition of a word or phrase/the use of adverbials such as on the other hand, in contrast, or as a consequence) • Know and use a wide range of words that would support cohesion, including the precise use of more complex connectives (e.g. nevertheless, moreover) • Varying levels of formality are adopted according to purpose and audience (appropriate use of controlled informality, shifts between formal narrative and informal dialogue) • A range of stylistic features contribute to the effect of the text (e.g. rhetorical questions, repetition and figurative language) • Verb forms are mostly controlled and are consistently adapted to the form of writing (It would be helpful if you could let me know, as this will enable me to take further action.)	Use a wide range of well controlled punctuation for effect, meaning and pace **Terminology for pupils** precision and impact cohesive devices formality

Appendix 2 – Word class cards

Nouns (copy on to blue paper) – naming word

baby	girl	fish
man	teacher	book
mountain	river	dog
dinosaur	Jack	tiger
Ice-cream	car	crowd
family	thieves	bird
feet	team	pencil

Pronouns (copy on to pale blue paper) – replaces a noun

she	I	ours
he	they	it

Verbs (copy on to red paper) – doing or being word

fell	screamed	walked
scored	cried	won
swam	played	watched
jumped	laughed	shouted
flew	ran	cartwheeled
roared	pounced	sang
broke	barked	stank

Adjectives (copy on to green paper) – describing

bright	short	huge
dull	green	excellent
blue	timid	treacherous
frail	little	boisterous
brave	brilliant	frightening
horrible	delicious	white
large	dazzling	old
hungry	armoured	fast

Adverbs (copy on to yellow paper) – how an action is performed

slowly	loudly	clearly
quickly	suddenly	clumsily
awkwardly	carefully	horribly
cautiously	terribly	loudly
finally	quietly	beautifully
stupidly	happily	rapidly
immediately	politely	sleepily

Articles (copy on to lilac paper) – signposts an object is about to be mentioned

a	a	the
the	an	the

Conjunctions (copy on to light yellow paper) – joining words

meanwhile	as long as	whenever
if	so	while
until	since	when
as	when	after
even though	although	because
because	therefore	who
with	if	although
unless	until	in case

Prepositions (copy on to pink paper) – positional words

in	into	through
over	on	under
beside	to	across
underneath	below	from
with	down	before
after	in front of	between

Punctuation marks (copy on to white paper)

Cap	Cap	
?	!	-
,	"	"
:	;	,

Glossary

Adjective: An adjective is a word used to describe or modify a noun, *e.g. sharp, fluffy, warm, dry, expensive.* They can be made **comparative** by adding –er, *e.g. bigger* or **superlative** by adding est, *biggest.*

Adverb: These describe or modify words other than nouns and often end in –ly. They usually indicate how (e.g. carefully), when (e.g. finally), where (e.g. outside), how often (rarely), or why (e.g. accidentally) something happens.

Adverbial phrase: An adverbial phrase is a group of related words which play the role of an adverb. Like all phrases, an adverbial phrase does not include a subject and a verb. Commonly they describe where, when or how something happened *e.g. In the middle of the night. . . .*

Alliteration: The repetition of a sound at the beginning of words, *e.g. kicking cats.*

Apostrophe: Shows either that letters have been omitted, e.g. *cannot – can't* or to show the possessive form of a noun, e.g. *Harry's sister.*

Clauses: A group of words that includes a subject and a verb. A clause expresses a complete event or situation and usually contains a subject and a verb e.g. The **dog chased** me.

Cohesion: Refers to the underlying logic, consistency and flow of a text. Cohesive devices are words that make clear how a text's parts are related to one another. Pronouns, prepositions, adverbs and connectives are especially important for building cohesion, e.g. *Indi turned round and looked into the bushes. Just then, she heard a strange noise.* The phrase just then helps relate the events in time.

Colloquial language: Everyday, spoken-style language containing words that are commonly understood e.g. *she's out* for *she is not at home.*

Colons (:): These should be used to introduce a list or show a link between the units of meaning. Use a colon to punctuate the end of a sentence when a list of items follows, e.g. The class will expose you to the following topics: politics, history and economics.

Comma (,): A punctuation mark used to help the reader by separating parts of a sentence. They are used to mark the divisions in sentences, as may be caused by phrases, clauses or conjunctions. Commas are also used to separate list items.

Complex sentence: A complex sentence comprises one independent clause and at least one subordinate clause.

Compound sentence: This will contain at least two independent clauses. The two clauses are joined together using a coordinating conjunction which is used when you want to give equal emphasis to two main clauses. The acronyms FANBOYS can be used to remember the coordinating conjunctions: for, and, nor, but, or, yet, so, e.g.
- John threw a ball **and** the dog ran to get it.
- My cat loves being stoked **but** hates having his claws cut.
- She had to work late **so** she could not go to the cinema.
- Let's meet at the cinema **or** by the clock tower.

Conjunction: A word used to link clauses within a sentence, *e.g. The dog barked but the cat stood its ground.*

Connective: A word that joins ideas together. Connectives can be conjunctions (eg *but, when, because*) or connecting adverbs, e.g. *however, then, therefore.*

Dash (–): Used especially in informal writing to replace other punctuation marks, i.e. colons, semi-colons, commas or brackets e.g. *He can't afford it – the tickets alone were too expensive.*

Determiner: Stands before a noun and any other words that modify the noun, *e.g. a, the, this, any, my.*

Direct and indirect speech: In direct speech, we use the speaker's original words e.g. 'Quickly!' he called, 'we must leave before the dragon finds us.' Rules for speech:
- Put the speech marks round what is actually said and start the speech with a capital letter, e.g. 'I'll be back soon,' Amy shouted.
- Separate the direct speech from the rest of the sentence, usually using a comma: Lily said quietly, 'Please sit down.'

- Punctuate inside the speech marks. If the speech comes first use a comma, (unless a question or exclamation mark is needed) as the sentence is not completed e.g. 'If you're not gone when the three days have passed, we will feast,' the cave witch warned with an evil glint in her eye.
- Sometimes you can break the direct speech up by inserting information. This is the only time when you do not use a capital letter for the first word inside the speech marks e.g. 'If you think you can speak to me like that,' Amir said, 'you had better think again!'
- Start a new line for a new speaker.
- Don't overuse speech. It should be used to develop either the characters or plot.

Indirect (or reported) speech is used to report what was said but do not use the exact words of the original speaker. Typically we change pronouns and verb tenses, and speech marks are not used, e.g. *Sarah said* **that she had better** *sit down.*

Edit: To modify written work through checking and making improvements in relation to words, sentences and text organisation and cohesion. This takes place after drafting, and before proofreading (a final check of spelling errors and punctuation).

Ellipsis (. . .): Three dots used for a pause or to show that words have been left out.

Homophones: Two words with the same pronunciation e.g. *hear* and *here*.

Idiom: A common phrase or saying, *e.g. Pull your socks up.*

Nominalisation: Abstract nouns derived from verbs. e.g. discover – discovery, explore – exploration.

Nouns: A word used to name a thing, a person, a place etc. As a general rule, it is something that you can put the word 'the' in front of. E.g. chair, person, house, weather, moon, river, plate, etc. . .
- Proper nouns: begin with a capital letter and refer to specific people, places, occasions, etc. e.g. Tom, Manchester, Tuesday.
- Concrete nouns: Refer to physical things like people, objects and places.
- Abstract nouns: refer to things that do not exist physically, e.g. feelings, ideas, qualities, e.g. happiness, friendship.
- Collective nouns: refer to groups of people, animals or objects, e.g. family, flock.

Noun phrase: A group of words which act like a noun. Words can go before the noun, e.g. *The ferocious dog.* Or after the noun, *The field overgrown with nettles.* They modify the meaning of the noun.

Object: A noun or pronoun that is being acted on by a verb e.g. The boy kicked **the ball**. The subject of the sentence is the boy.

Parts of speech: Traditional grammar classifies words based on eight **parts of speech**: the verb, the noun, the pronoun, the adjective, the adverb, the preposition, the conjunction and determiner.

Passive voice: This is used where the thing receiving the action is placed first and the thing doing the action is optionally included near the end of the sentence:
- *The boy kicked the ball.* Active: the subject is placed first.
- *The ball was kicked by the boy.* Passive: the object receiving the action is placed first.

Personification: When an animal or inanimate object is described as having human characteristics e.g. *The tree leaned menacingly over the river.*

Phrases: Two or more words functioning as a unit in a sentence. Phrases do not have verbs in them.

Prepositions: A word like *at, over, by* and *with* which is placed before a noun to show its relationship to something else in the sentence, e.g. She shouted **to** Jack and watched as he disappeared **into** the mist **at** the bottom **of** the woods.

Pronouns: Words used to replace a noun, e.g. *me, him, he, his, himself, who, what, that*

Relative subordinate clause: Starts with a pronoun e.g. who, which, that. *The boy, who was always very forgetful, left his jumper behind.*

Semi-colons(;) are useful in long sentences, but be careful not to over-use them. They give a longer pause than a comma, but not as long as a full stop. They are typically used to separate items in a list, e.g. In the library, there were several students reading journal articles; a couple of lecturers checking the stock; and a librarian returning books to the shelves.
- To provide a break in a sentence, while showing the relationship between the two parts. For example: Night was falling; he knew all was lost.
- To express an idea which is too short to merit a new sentence. For example: Wherever possible, students should try to organise their academic work by using 'planning tools'; these can help to clarify ideas.

Sentence: A group of words that expresses a complete thought. A sentence must contain a verb and usually a subject, e.g. He ran. (He – subject/ran – verb). There are four main sentence types:

- Declarative: convey information or make statements, e.g. Gok plays the guitar.
- Interrogative: ask questions, e.g. Is this your pen?
- Imperative: used to issue orders or directives, e.g. Hang your coat on the peg.
- Exclamative: used to make a more forceful version of a sentence e.g. I am not eating it!

Similes and metaphors: A simile is where two things are directly compared because they share a common feature. The word as or like is used to compare the two words, e.g. As cold as a dog's nose. A metaphor also compares two things, but it does so more directly without using as or like, e.g. The shop was a little gold-mine.

Simple sentence: Made up of one clause, e.g. the dog barked.

Subject/verb agreement: Subjects and verbs must agree with one another.

- In some cases the form of verb changes according to the subject, e.g. *I am/he is/they are/ I was/you were*.
- The verb changes if it is in the third or first person, e.g. *I like / She likes*.
- If a subject is singular, its verb must also be singular e.g. The dog **chases** the cat / The dogs chase the cats.
- There are some cases where a determiner must agree with a noun, e.g. *this pen, these pens*.

Subordinate clauses: Begin with a subordinate conjunction or a relative pronoun and will contain both a subject and a verb. This combination of words will *not* form a complete sentence. It will instead make a reader want additional information e.g. *As Paul hauled his sack through the busy streets,* he noticed the dense fog swirling round the lamp-posts.

Subordinate conjunctions: These come at the beginning of a subordinate clause: e.g. after, although, as, because, before, even though, if.

Verbs: Describe an action (e.g. He **chased** . . .), an occurrence / happening (e.g. The snow **glistened**.) or a state of being, (*e.g. I know . . .)* There are two main types of verbs:

- Lexical verbs are the main verb in the sentence. All verbs include a lexical verb e.g. Sam **ran** up the path.
- Auxiliary verbs help the main verb e.g. Sam **has** taken the dog for a walk. Modal verbs are types of auxiliary verb that express degree of possibility e.g. could, might.

Verb inflections: Verbs can be inflected for tense:

- Infinitive: the base form of the verb without any additional endings, *e.g. to play*.
- Present tense: describe actions in the present, *e.g. I go, I am going, they are going*.
- Past tense: normally formed by adding –ed (happened) but many verbs have irregular forms e.g. sink – sank, sunk.
- Present participle is used to express an active action and is formed by adding -ing e.g. running, being.
- Future tense – English has no 'future tense' but can be marked in a number of ways, all of which include a present-tense verb, *e.g. they will break*.
- Finite verb: shows tense, person or singular plural. Finite verbs are important because a written sentence normally needs at least one clause that contains a finite verb, and a finite verb must have an explicit subject, *e.g, I go, she goes, he went*.
- Continuous verb: Describes ongoing actions. It is formed by taking the *–ing* form of the verb and adding words such as *was, am, will be, e.g. he was reading or he has been reading*.
- Perfect tense: Describes finished actions and are normally formed by adding had, have or has in front of the past tense e.g. *I had gone, He has gone, I will have gone*. It can also be combined with the continuous, *e.g. he has been reading*.

References

Alexander Robin, et al, (2009) *Children, their World, their Education*, Final Report and Recommendations of the Cambridge Primary Review (Routledge)

Andrews R, Torgerson C, Beverton S, Freeman A, Locke T, Low G, Robinson A, Zhu D (2004) *The effect of grammar teaching (sentence combining) in English on 5 to 16 year olds' accuracy and quality in written composition*: Review summary. (University of York, UK)

Andrews R, Torgerson C, Beverton S, Freeman A, Locke T, Low G, Robinson A, Zhu D (2005) *The effect of grammar teaching on writing development.* (Routledge)

Beard Roger, *The Effective Teaching of Writing,* TOPIC – Practical applications of research in education. Issue 26, Autumn 2001.

Bew Lord, (2011) *Independent Review of Key Stage 2 testing, assessment and accountability* (Department for Education)

Black P and Wiliam D, (1990) *Inside the Black Box: Raising Standards Through Classroom Assessment* (Granada Learning)

Blatchford P, Bassett P, Brown P, Martin C, Russell A, Webster R, (2007) *Deployment and Impact of Support Staff in Schools* (Institute of Education, University of London, Department for Children, Schools and Families)

Cambridge Primary Review (2009) Routledge

Clarke, Shirley, (2003) *Enriching feedback in the primary classroo*m (Hodder)

Corbett Pie, (2008) Storytelling (The National Strategies/Primary)

Dale, Edgar (1948) *Audio-Visual Methods in Teaching* (The Drydan Press)

Department for Children, Schools and Families (2007) *Primary Framework, Improving writing with a focus on guided writing*

Department for Employment and Education (2000) *Grammar for Writing*

Department for Education (2013) *Primary Assessment and Accountability Under the New National Curriculum*

Department for Education, (2013) *The National Curriculum in England Key stages 1 and 2 framework document (*2013)

Education Standards Research Team (2012) *What is the research evidence on writing?* (Department for Education)

Excellence in English, What we can learn from 12 outstanding schools (2011) (Ofsted)

Harris, R J. (1962) *'An experimental inquiry into the functions and value of formal grammar in the teaching of English, with special reference to the teaching of correct written English to children aged 12 to 14'* unpublished thesis (University of London)

Hart B and Risley T (1995) 'The Early Catastrophe. The 30 Million Word Gap by Age 3' published in *Meaningful Differences in the Everyday Experiences of Young American* Children (Brookes)

Higgins S, Kokotsaki D and Coe R (2011) *Toolkit of Strategies to Improve Learning: Summary for Schools* (Sutton Trust)

Holt John, (1991) *How Children Learn* (Penguin)

Kirby J, (2013) *What we can learn from core knowledge and ED Hirsch*

Letters and Sounds (2007) (Department for Education and Skills)

Moore R, (2002) in *'Literacy and Learning',* Issue 24, March/April 2002 (Questions Publishing, UK)

Myhill et al, (2012) in *What is the Research Evidence on Writing?* Department for Education

National Curriculum (2009)*APP writing standards file: Kylie* (Department for Education)

Primary National Strategy (2006) *Primary Framework for literacy and mathematics* (Department for Education and Skills)

Ofsted (2009) *English at the crossroads: an evaluation of English in primary and secondary schools*

Ofsted (2012) *Moving English Forward*

Ofsted,(1999) *National Literacy Strategy: an interim evaluation*

Ofsted (2000) *The Teaching of Writing in primary schools: Could do better* – A discussion paper

O'Hare, F. (1973). *Sentence combining: Improving student writing without formal grammar instruction* (NCTE Research Report No. 15). Urbana, IL: NCTE

Palmer Sue (2003) *How to Teach Writing Across the Curriculum at Key Stage 1 (Writers' Workshop)* (Routledge)

Qualifications and Curriculum Authority (1998) *The Grammar Papers* (QCA publications)

The Sutton Trust (2011) *Spending the Pupil Premium* 2011)

Standards and Testing Agency (2012) *English Grammar, Punctuation and Spelling Test*

Standards and Testing Agency (2013) *English Grammar, Punctuation and Spelling Test Performance Descriptors*

Standards and Testing Agency,(2013) *Glossary of terms: Key Stage 2 English grammar, punctuation and spelling test*

Standards and Testing Agency (2013) *Key Stage 2 Writing exemplification*

Tandy M and Howell J (2008) *Creating Writers in the Primary Classroom* (David Fulton)

Wray D. and Lewis M. (1995) *Developing children's non-fiction writing Scholastic*

Wray D and Medwell J, (1997) *Teaching English in primary schools: Handbook of Lesson Plans, Knowledge and Teaching Methods* Letts, UK

Wyse D, (2001) *Grammar for Writing? A Critical Review of Empirical Evidence,* The British Journal of Educational Studies, Vol 49, Dec 2001